W9-BSI-887

RENEWING OUR MINISTRY

RENEWING OUR MINISTRY

David L. McKenna

WORD BOOKS
PUBLISHER
WACO, TEXAS

A DIVISION OF
WORD, INCORPORATED

Library of Congress Cataloging-in-Publication Data

McKenna, David L. (David Loren), 1929–
  Renewing our ministry.

  1. Pastoral theology.   I. Title.
BV4011.M44   1986   253   85–26382
ISBN 0–8499–0500–1

6 7 8 9 B K C 9 8 7 6 5 4 3 2 1

To
Janet, my wife,
and
Rob, my son,
who not only survived a change
of worlds with me, but have served
as God's personal agents for my daily renewal.

Contents

Introduction

$\mathbf{W}$e who are pastors live in a fishbowl and work in a test-tube. In the fishbowl we are constantly under the scrutiny of the public eye. In the test-tube we are perpetually under the analysis of the researcher's pen. Consequently, everyone has an opinion or a statistic that tells us what's wrong with the pastoral ministry. Horror stories reinforce statistics about pastoral flame-out, burnout and drop-out. The result is a loss of confidence in the clergy, especially among the young. A Gallup poll of religious attitudes of teenagers shows that 90 percent believe in God, 70 percent attend church, 50 percent consider religion very important in their lives and 40 percent pray regularly—but only 25 percent have strong confidence in the clergy!

As an ordained minister and a seminary president, I see the ministry both subjectively and objectively. Readers of this book will soon realize that I am a cheerleader for pastors. Whatever our flaws, I can never forget that pastors are called of God and anointed by the Holy Spirit to preach the glorious gospel of Jesus Christ.

Billy Graham illustrates my conviction. At a presidential prayer breakfast during the late 1960s in Washington, D.C., I heard him defend, with Scripture, the American policy of fire bombing in Vietnam. For several years I harbored the notion that he had been seduced by political power at the expense of the gospel. Then, at the Lausanne Conference on Evangelization in 1974, God's Spirit taught me otherwise.

The closing public rally of the Congress took place in the soccer stadium at Lausanne. Murphy's Law ruled the setting and the service. Due to the sanctity with which the Swiss hold their soccer turf, the crowd of more than 30,000 people was separated from the speaker's rostrum by the width of the field and the running track on both sides. From a communications standpoint, the distance eliminated any opportunity for eye contact or voice intimacy. To add to the frustration, the planning committee overscheduled the preliminaries, which included prolonged testimonies by three international delegates who spoke through interpreters.

Almost two-and-a-half hours after the service began, Billy Graham took the pulpit to preach. He had come from a week in bed, under a doctor's care, just for the occasion. Although his sermon, under the hot sun, was mercifully short, it qualified as a disaster. He read the wrong scripture, losing his place time and again as the wind blew his notes. He struggled against his sickness for the strength and vitality which characterized his preaching.

As one who has suffered through similar experiences, my heart went out to him, but my mind wrote off the service as a total loss. So when Billy had the audacity to give an altar call, I squinted at the blurred masses in the distant bleachers and concluded, "No one will come." I forgot the work of the Holy Spirit. As the strains of "Just As I Am" echoed through the air, at least 900 people filed out of the stands and filled up the running track on the opposite side of the field. At that moment I bowed my head and acknowledged that Billy Graham, whatever his flaws, was God's anointed man. Since then, if you want an argument about Billy's statements, decisions or travels, you will get my answer, "He may not be perfect, but he is anointed."

My experience as a seminary president extends my conclusion about Billy Graham to all pastors who are called of God and anointed by His Spirit to preach the gospel. As an educator with high expectations for academic achievement, I might wish for more brilliance and breadth among the prospects for pastoral ministry. As a psychologist with some understanding of personality, I might wonder about the security and maturity of many who claim the call to preach. As a churchman with a vision for a lost world, I might yearn for more creative risk-takers for the leadership of the future. But then, the Holy Spirit checks me with the reminder that Jesus chose twelve of the most unlikely people to be His disciples. From this perspective, the potential for ministry is unlimited.

Therefore, as a seminary president, I bear the "weight of glory" about which C. S. Lewis preached. In every seminarian I look for the gift of God which can be developed into a special instrument for effective ministry. The development of this gift cannot be accomplished apart from the work of the Holy Spirit. For this reason, we at Asbury continue to emphasize the doctrine, experience, discipline and practice of perfect love which Jesus promised with the coming of the Holy Spirit. Experience has taught us that without the pervasive depths and the enhancing reach of the Holy Spirit, our ministry is vain. But with the help of the Holy Spirit, the surprises are endless. Our ministry is extended and enhanced far beyond our qualifications, expectations and circumstances.

In this book we claim the same promise and invoke the same principle for the renewal of our ministry. Those who are ready to criticize the ministry or cancel out the effectiveness of pastors forget the resources of the Holy Spirit precommitted to the disciples of Jesus Christ and especially His ministers of the gospel. Beginning with our calling to ministry, progressing through our ongoing tasks and projecting forward into our promising future, the purpose of this book is singular. *God in Christ, through His Holy Spirit, has precommitted all of the resources we need for the renewal of our ministry.* Thus, this is a good news book reflecting the thoughts of one who is a pastor, a love story written by one who has never lost the thrill of preaching and an autobiographical journal of one who knows and still needs renewal. My prayer is that every minister of the gospel who reads this book will kneel in the presence of God, claim the promises for renewal and rise with an energizing gleam in the eye given by the Spirit of God.

Thank God for the agents of renewal who are part of my life history—past and present. To represent the pastors who have served me, I single out Dr. Robert Fine, Senior Minister of the First Free Methodist Church in Seattle, Washington. When I was a young president of Seattle Pacific College (now University), during a time of transition when crisis and doubt became the order of the day, his sermons had the insights and his counsel had the wisdom to see me through. But I best remember him as a stately, spiritual presence upon whom I could lean. Dr. Fine died an early death, but not without leaving me the memory of a source of strength in my time of need.

Even as I write, I mourn the loss of another agent of renewal in my life. News has just come about the death of Dr. Hugh A. White, Chairman of the Board of Trustees of Spring Arbor College (Michigan). Early in my career, Dr. White put his confidence in me. The test came when he invited me to be the president of Spring Arbor College. I was only thirty-one. During the next seven years he taught me how to grow people by growing me—a smile of approval, a word of caution, a question of challenge, a prayer of praise—but always with space to grow. Just to be with him was to be renewed.

Still another giant in my life is Dr. Phillip Ashton, former Dean and Professor of Psychology at Seattle Pacific University. In 1968 God called us to make the transcontinental move from Spring Arbor, Michigan, to Seattle, Washington, 2500 miles from our parents and families. With four children, including a five-week-old baby, and a pesky white poodle, we moved. Dr. Ashton had already retired from teaching but he and his wife, Flo, graced every event of the campus and church with their regal silver-haired presence. Sensing our need for family and still hurting from the loss of their only child, they adopted us. As an example of how the body of Christ creates new families, Dr. and Mrs. Ashton are "Dad" and "Mom" for us and our children.

Finally, I recall an experience with Lloyd John Ogilvie, which stands out as a peak experience of pastoral renewal for me. In 1985 he came to Asbury Theological Seminary as the guest speaker for our annual Ministers' Conference. To some, Dr. Ogilvie might seem to be a star-studded Christian celebrity with the glamor and gloss of his Hollywood ministry. If that image exists, it is false. Lloyd Ogilvie is a pastor to pastors without peer. After he won the confidence of 800 ministers and spouses at our Conference with sound biblical preaching, the atmosphere became charged with the need for renewal as pastors asked for an altar call. Deeply moved and fully sensitive to the Holy Spirit, Dr. Ogilvie asked how he could minister to the pastors' needs in the closing service. Finally, he took the risk of asking that twenty wounded pastors come to the front of the auditorium for a prayer of healing. One by one he went to them, heard their confession, laid hands on them and prayed for them. Then he asked the twenty "wounded healers" to turn around and become pastors to others who were equally wounded. Line after line of pastors and spouses filled the aisles. Almost two hours later, Dr. Ogilvie stood praying with the last person who came to him. He missed his lunch and his airplane to be an agent of renewal among us. Before he left, I asked that he also minister to me—pastor to pastor.

After twenty-five consecutive years in three presidencies—a college, a university and a seminary—I am asked how I survive and stay fresh. My answer is that I am having fun doing God's will. People around me make the difference—the trustees who show confidence in me, the faculty who consider me a colleague, the students who think of me as a friend and an office staff which thrives in a pressure cooker of presidential decisions, public demands and publisher's deadlines. Without Sheila Lovell, my executive assistant, who has the gift of an author and the skill of an editor, Lois Mulcahy, my secretary, who has not only mastered the word processor but turned production into a ministry, and Christy Beatty, who complements her position as vice-president of the student body with work-study hours for a search-and-discovery mission among the speeches and articles of the president's office, this book would have remained buried in the files under the category of "things to be done." Their loyalty and labor, love and laughter keep me renewed.

RENEWING OUR MINISTRY

I

Reliving Our Call

Ministry is like marriage. It is an intensely intimate relationship between two persons in which passionate romance captures the affections, a long-term dream focuses the mind and sacred vows seal the will. Of course, neither ministry nor marriage is without changing circumstances and periodic crises. In a lifetime of ministry or marriage, passions will rise and fall; dreams will move in and out of focus. More often than not, the time will come when only the eternal commitment, ". . . till death do us part," will hold ministry or marriage together. Then, as the commitment is relived, the romance is rekindled and the dream is renewed.

Do you remember the romance, the dream and the call that brought you into ministry? My call came as a high school junior seeking God's will through the searching of His Word. For the first time, I read, "How beautiful are the feet of those who preach the gospel of peace, who bring glad tidings of good things" (Rom. 10:15).

3

An indescribable thrill pulsated through my soul. Romantic that I am, I fell in love with ministry. Before me, I saw the vision of a preaching career affirmed by the promises of a "beautiful," "glad" and "good" life. Then and there, I answered God's call and spoke my vow to be His minister.

Do you remember the turning points in your career when your romance with ministry was rekindled, your dream was renewed and your vows were repeated? My ministerial career now spans thirty-five years and includes preaching, teaching, administration, scholarship and public service. Along the way there have been several turning points. Choices have been made between pastor and professor, professor and president, president and politician. At each intersection, the call, "How beautiful are the feet of those who preach the gospel of peace, who bring glad tidings of good things," has come back to me with all the passion of my original romance, all of the anticipation of my original dream and all of the sacredness of my original vow.

Some of the turning points stand out as critical. An invitation came to be the president of a prestigious foundation. While I prayed and pondered the opportunity, three questions formed in my mind,

How can I minister?
How can I lead?
How can I create?

These three questions pose the priorities of a lifetime— my call to be a minister of the gospel, my career as a Christian college president and my need to be a builder on the cutting edge of the kingdom. Putting the invitation to be president of the foundation to this threefold test, I determined that I could minister in the role by directing significant financial resources toward Christian outreach, but I could not lead or create because the trustees wanted a manager to implement their policies, not a leader to initiate proposals for policy. A few years later, another invitation came to pioneer an imaginative communications venture in world evangelism. Each of the three test questions received a resounding "Yes" until the chairman of the board misread my motives and added the incentive, "Furthermore, I'll give you a bonus that will make you a millionaire in ten years!" He had tipped his hand. I knew that if push came to shove in the decisions between dollars and souls, the profit motive would dominate. On the airplane heading home, an unspeakable joy surged through me as I remembered the bonus that went with my original calling—a "beautiful," "glad" and "good" life. With a lighthearted freedom that I have seldom known, I wrote in my daybook, "I'd rather be a minister than a millionaire."

Still later, the possibility of a position in the president's cabinet of the United States came into view. Far beyond my fondest or wildest dreams, I wanted the position. Still, I prayed half-heartedly, "Lord, if I cannot minister, lead and create in that high post, don't let me have it." The appointment process went down to the wire before capricious political winds left me with the small satisfaction of being able to tell my grandchildren that I came in "second." Although I'll never know the answer for sure, I suspect that my tenure as Secretary of Education would have been short in a setting when the first rule of survival is, "Keep your head down and your mouth shut."

God is not only wise, but subtle. While I was still trying to understand why He led me so far down the track toward a Christian witness in the secular setting of federal government, He put a "U-turn" in my career. An invitation came to consider the presidency of Asbury Theological Seminary. Except for my original calling to be a minister and my loving relationship as an alumnus of the Seminary, my ministerial career had been almost exclusively in the field of administration in Christian colleges and universities. Still, the Spirit of God nudged me to consider the invitation. In the painful and prayerful process of decision-making, I relived my original calling. A sense of "coming home" overtook me as I thought about putting theological and spiritual

shoes on the "beautiful feet" of a new generation of ministers who are called to "preach the glad tidings of good
things." Almost like the spark of first love, my romance
with ministry in the pastoral setting of the local church
and the evangelistic thrust of a world mission caught fire.

Simultaneously, I spoke the same sacred vow that sealed
my lifetime commitment to ministry, "Not my will, but
thine be done." In the days that followed, a new dream
came into focus. Through the mind of the Spirit, I saw
the potential of Asbury Theological Seminary fulfilling the
visionary reach of John Wesley who boldly declared, "The
world is my parish." Rather than seeing Asbury as an institution stuck at the end of a rural road on the edge of Appala-
chia, God showed me a crossroads for the Wesleyan and
evangelical world from which the gospel of peace would
be taken as He commanded, ". . . unto the ends of the
earth." All of the diverse components of my career in the
Christian university, the secular community and the evangelical world converged in that dream as preparation for
bringing new vision and vitality to a seminary poised on
strong foundations for a leap into the future.

You will not be surprised then, to learn that my first
address to the students at Asbury Theological Seminary
was entitled, "The Call to Ministry." My purpose was to
fix in the students' minds the common call of Jesus to each
generation of ministry, "Follow Me, and I will make you
fishers of men" (Matt. 4:19). Nor will you be surprised to
know that God has called me to the "ministry of encouragement" for pastors, educators, evangelists and missionaries
wherever I go to preach and teach. If self-esteem is a problem among ministers, I am an antidote. To me, there is
no higher calling than to preach the gospel of peace. To
me, there is no better journey than the one walked by the
"beautiful feet" of the minister. To me, there is no greater
joy than to bring to sad and sinful people "glad tidings of
good things."

Twenty-five years ago, at the green and tender age of

thirty-one, I became the youngest college president in the nation. With such a dubious and short-lived honor comes the danger of peaking early and fading fast. Not so for the minister of God. The steps are ever-forward, the horizon is ever-opening and the vision is ever-lengthening. Therefore, we go from peak to peak with the highest level still ahead of us. From that vista, I can testify as an example of God's promise, "He who calls you is faithful, who also will do it" (1 Thess. 5:24). Again, again and again, on the road and at the intersections of our career, by rekindling the romance, refocusing the dream and reminding us of our vows, God renews our ministry.

II

Remembering Our Commitment

Ministry is a self-giving role, a twenty-four-hour-a-day task and a fishbowl existence. The drain upon physical, emotional and spiritual resources is constant. Thus, every minister who is worthy of the name will confess flat spots and dry spells. Unless there is renewal, tragic consequences follow—emotional burnout, occupational dropout or ecclesiastical turnout. None of these symptoms of stress represents God's intention for the prized people from whom He asks total commitment. His promise is renewal. Therefore, when our romance with ministry wanes or our dream for ministry dulls, God's alternative to "burnout," "dropout" or "turnout" is an invitation to remember *why* Christ calls us to the ministry and to reclaim the resources of His promise for renewal.

Jesus opens His public ministry with the dramatic declaration:

> The time is fulfilled, and
> the kingdom of God is at hand.
> Repent,
>   and
> believe in the gospel.
>   (Mark 1:15)

Immediately, then, Jesus journeys to a fishing village alongside the Sea of Galilee in search of help. Even Jesus knows that He cannot do His job alone. More than that, He knows that the preaching of the gospel is a risk that can mean His life. Jesus needs friends whom He can trust, disciples whom He can teach and co-workers with whom He can share His task.

Simon and Andrew, brothers in the fishing business, appear to be the most ordinary and unlikely candidates for ministry. Yet Jesus calls out to them, "Come after Me, and I will make you become fishers of men" (Mark 1:17).

Immediately they respond. Throwing down their nets and turning away from the guaranteed future of their father's fishing business, they follow the stranger who offers nothing more than the hope and hazards of angling for the souls of men. In them Jesus sees the potential for ministerial leadership—friends who are trustworthy, disciples who are teachable and co-workers who are task-oriented.

Every minister of the gospel hears the same call and receives the same promise. However God individualizes His invitation to fit the person and the circumstances, each call is a variation on the theme, "Come after Me, and I will make you become fishers of men." What an honor! In this call is a reminder that Jesus chooses us because He still needs friends who are *trustworthy*, disciples who are *teachable* and co-workers who are *task-oriented*. To remember the honor of our calling and reclaim the resources of His promise is to be renewed for ministry again and again.

To Be Trustworthy

When Jesus goes to the fishing village to call out disciples to whom He will leave the responsibility for leading the church and winning the world, He takes the greatest gamble in history. The qualifications of Simon and Andrew are minimal but they have one essential quality for ministry—they are *trustworthy*. Perhaps from their survival skills on a fishing boat during a storm at sea or from the rigorous requirements for success in the fishing business, Simon and Andrew know the meaning of mutual trust, faith and loyalty. When Jesus calls, "Come," they come.

Management theorists might say that the lowly fishermen were attracted by the charisma of Jesus' personality and wanted to be identified with Him (personal faith). Or perhaps they were simply seeking. They heard credibility in His call and saw the potential for learning at His feet (rational faith). Still others might suggest that Simon and Andrew were motivated by the promise of the reward to become "fishers of men" (instrumental faith). Whatever the reason for their response, the call of Jesus is clear. He sees in them the quality of trust upon which friendship, discipleship and leadership can be built.

Wonder of wonders! God needs us. As contradictory as it seems, the all-sufficient God calls insufficient men and women to do His sovereign will and achieve His good purpose. Once and for all, Jesus buries the arrogance of leaders who assume that they need no one to help them.

Back in the time when pipe organs were pumped manually, the concert stage was blessed and cursed by a prima donna of the organ keyboard whose ego knew no bounds. Primping and preening before he played, he found his audience tolerating his behavior only because his artistry canceled out the repulsive parade of his egotistical whims.

One night, however, his arrogance got out of hand. Endlessly he spoke of his accomplishments and laid claim to being the organist without peer in the world. Finally he got around to his performance. With one last flourish of his tuxedo tails and one more pretentious adjustment of the organ bench, he raised his hands to play. His fingers attacked the keyboard with undaunted artistic confidence, but instead of thunderous sound . . . *nothing!* A grimace and a weak smile accompanied the raising of his hands once again. With even more dramatic flair he brought his hands down on the keyboard. Again . . . *nothing!* Enraged and snorting like a bull, the organist bolted from the bench and stormed behind the stage, where a grubby urchin pumped the bellows. "You oaf!" he screamed, "What have you done? You have ruined the master's performance!" Casually munching an apple at his place before the bellows, the boy looked up and chided him, "Say, 'We,' mister. Say 'We.' "

If anyone has the right and power to say, "I," it is Jesus. Yet He sets the tone and cuts the pattern for all future Christian leadership by choosing to say "We" when He first calls Simon and Andrew to be His disciples. His reasons are a lesson in leadership.

Jesus needs trustworthy friends on whom He can count for personal support. Leadership is a lonely role. When all is said and done, a leader must make decisions that will make some people mad and some people glad. Abraham Lincoln once said, "When I make an appointment to a high office from among ten candidates, I make nine enemies and one ingrate." Billy Martin, the always fiery and often fired baseball manager, once described a successful baseball coach as the one who keeps the five players who hate him away from the four who are still uncertain. Even Jesus needs trustworthy friends to bolster His spirit when He is unjustly criticized and equally trustworthy friends to remind Him of His mission when praise gets out of hand.

Looking back over twenty-five years as a Christian college, university and seminary president, I put a premium upon loyalty among colleagues. In fact, my major crises have often been caused by breakdowns of loyalty. A vice-president for development cultivated a major donor and obtained a large capital gift for a new building. He refused, however, to transfer the personal loyalty that he had developed with the donor to me or to the institution. Therefore, when the vice-president left for another position, he took the donor's loyalty with him. In a sense, he made his own disciple and became a competitor with his president.

On another occasion, a candidate for a vice-presidency said that he put institutional loyalty above personal loyalty. At first blush, this sounds right. Later I learned that this idea of loyalty is the making of the "Judas Syndrome." When my decisions did not fit his interpretation of our institutional mission, he used "institutional loyalty" as a reason for betrayal.

On the other side of the ledger are people whose loyalty makes leadership worthwhile. For fourteen years I had an executive assistant known to everyone as "Cec." She served in the crossfire of the president's office. Vicious rumors, hateful letters, confidential memos and legal suits as well as angry people and sweet-talking solicitors came to her desk. Without the implicit and unswerving trust that existed between us, persons could have been destroyed, the institution damaged and the kingdom of God defaced. Yet, in all the years of our association there was never the slightest hint that she violated our trust. Although "Cec" was formally identified as my executive assistant, the truth is that she served as a leader in the ministry of trust.

Jesus also needs trustworthy friends to whom He can delegate His authority. Leaders who ask others to follow them and share their mission confront a unique dilemma. To get the job done through others they must delegate their authority but they cannot delegate their responsibility. A leader has to accept the full responsibility for the decisions and actions of those to whom authority is given. On my desk at this moment are letters from irate pastors and donors who are holding me responsible for an article written by a faculty member. Although I can write back to explain that I did not know about it, did not approve it and did not agree with it, such an answer is inadequate. Because the faculty member is under my authority, I am held responsible for his writing. In such cases, there is only one alternative to the frustration of becoming a dictator who censors such outbursts or a disciplinarian who chastises violators—the faculty member and I must have a mutual trust and share a common mission.

From this leadership perspective, we can better understand the risk that Jesus takes when He sends out the twelve disciples two by two with the authority to cast out demons, preach the gospel, heal the sick and shake the dust off their feet against those who refuse to receive or hear them (Mark 6:7–13). This field test is placed so early in Jesus' ministry that the disciples are still limited in their understanding of the gospel and relatively unskilled in its application to the complexities of sin and sickness. Because they go out with the authority of Jesus' name, their success or failure reflects directly back upon Him and remains His responsibility. What an example of trust at work! Jesus knows that even though they may stumble in their preaching and err in their healing, they will not abuse His authority or violate His confidence. He can trust them while He trains them.

Again, Jesus needs trustworthy friends to build His team. Loyalty is the glue that cements all human relationships. Peter, Simon and Andrew had learned loyalty as fishermen whose success and survival depended upon teamsmanship. Perhaps this is why Jesus called them first and held them in the circle of His closest confidence. At best, the twelve disciples of Jesus must have looked like a rag-tag army rather than a smooth-working and effective evangelistic team. The Gospels record their fierce rivalry as often as their fragile unity. But in the long run, with the exception of Judas who succumbed to self-interest, their common

loyalty to Jesus was sealed by the coming of the Holy
Spirit and they became the Great Commission team held
together in life and death by loyalty to their Lord Jesus
Christ.

*Finally, Jesus needs trustworthy friends to whom He can
transfer His leadership.* Sooner or later, leaders must face
the question of succession. They know that the acid test
of their leadership is their legacy to the future. Unless
their vision and values can be transferred to the next generation of leadership, their mission dies with them.

Some leaders become obsessed with their role in history.
Even among Christian ministries there are scrambles for
succession. We see founders of ministries trying to establish
a dynasty through a son, designate a colleague as heir ap-
parent, preserve a name through an educational institution
or write a book that is the *summum bonum* for a career.
For instance, this morning's newspaper carries the story
of a television preacher's secret plan to assure annual support of 200 million dollars to continue his ministry after
his death. In most cases, attempts to build a dynasty, ap-
point a successor, name an institution, write a book or preserve a program will fail because the glory goes to the wrong
person. With John the Baptist, the most successful of the
prophets, every minister who is true to the self-giving Christ
will say, "He must increase, but I must decrease" (John-
3:30).

Jesus has a particular problem of succession. He knows
that His time is severely limited and His disciples are mini-
mally qualified to succeed Him. Building upon the quality
of trust that He first sees in Simon and Andrew, He teaches
them what He can and tests them as time allows. But His
primary goal is to seal their faith in Him as the Christ.
His Word will be their authority, His works will be their
firsthand experience, His resurrection their indisputable
fact and His Holy Spirit their ever-present guide. With
full confidence, then, Jesus can transfer His leadership to
His disciples because they are trustworthy.

As a leader who depends upon trustworthy people, I understand how Jesus felt when Peter denied Him in the garden court. Later Peter reinforces that trust when he vows to Jesus, but before the rooster greets the dawn of the next day, he denies his Lord. Not a word is spoken when they pass in the hall of the Roman palace on crucifixion day. With the language of the eyes, Jesus speaks, "Peter, you betrayed our trust." One look was enough to send Peter out to repent with bitter tears.

Renewal for our ministry begins when we remember *why* Jesus calls us. He needs us and He trusts us. He needs us as friends who are loyal to Him; He trusts us as colleagues who will work with Him; He counts on us as heirs who will lead for Him. No higher honor can be given to us than to hear the call, "Come follow me . . . ." It is Christ complimenting us for being trustworthy.

To Be Teachable

Following the call for friends who are trustworthy, Jesus extends His invitation to Simon and Andrew with a promise, "Come after me, and *I will make you become. . . ."* His choice of the term "become" is intentional. [It is a term that implies the engagement of the student in a lifetime of learning and compliments the developmental potential of the student as a learner.] Simply put, Jesus calls for disciples who are *teachable.*

Oftentimes we think of fishermen as ignorant people. Nothing could be farther from the truth. Fishing is a science that requires intelligent actions; fishing is an art that requires intuitive understanding. Our local paper, *The Lexington Herald-Leader,* carried the lengthy obituary of a mountain preacher. His life of ministry in small Kentucky towns was matched by his reputation as a fisherman. Wherever he put his line into the water, fish would bite. Everyone wanted to learn from him and I suspect that he had as many converts along the bank of the river as he did at the altar of prayer. When asked to reveal his success as a fisherman, the preacher answered, "You have to learn to think like a fish." He might have been unschooled but he was not unlearned. So it is with the disciples whom Jesus calls.

To be teachable is to be open to learning. When Jesus sets forth the promise, "I will make you become . . . ." He invites Simon and Andrew into a lifelong learning and growth process that will lead to spiritual maturity. Not by accident, He calls for teachable people who do not have case-hardened intellectual perceptions about the coming of the Messiah or bedrock prejudices about the nature of the kingdom of God. He puts into practice an axiom of educational psychology: *It is easier to learn than to unlearn.*

Do you remember the story about the bishop kneeling all alone at the altar in the front of the church? A young minister came into the back of the sanctuary, saw him and exclaimed, "What an example! The Bishop is seeking the wisdom of God." His calloused companion in the ministry who stood beside him scoffed, "Don't kid yourself. He is just rearranging his prejudices." Jesus does not call His ministers into a learning process that is nothing more than a rearrangement of prejudices. He calls for teachable people who have nothing to unlearn about the theology of the kingdom of God, the principles of holy living or the promise of the Savior. Too much time is lost if Jesus has to "deprogram our prejudices" before He can teach us His way. We are called to ministry because we are open to learning.

To be teachable is to be subject to discipline. When Jesus says to Simon and Andrew, "*I will make you become. . . .*" He calls them into the root meaning of the word "education" which is to "educe." An analogy illustrates "education" at work. Imagine a tool-and-die making process in which molten metal is drawn through a small hole in a fire-resistant die to form a useful wire or tool after the metal is cooled. This is the education process which is like the discipline of learning. We can think of our ministry the same way. The heat of the crucible is the intensity of our ministerial task; the malleability of the metal is our openness to learning; the shaping of the die represents the discipline of the Holy Spirit; the stretching of the metal is the pain of our learning, but there is no alternative if we are to "become" an instrument whom God can use for effective ministry.

To be teachable is to be willing to take a risk. When Jesus calls Simon and Andrew to be His disciples, He takes the risk of putting His plan for winning the world into the hands of faulty and flawed human beings. In turn, He asks them to be risk-takers too. They will have to give up their guaranteed security as successors in their father's fishing business for an uncertain future following in the footsteps of a carpenter's son. Perhaps the hazards of their occupation as fishermen prepared them for the risk-taking. In another instance when Jesus calls out to a man, "Follow me," the response comes back, "Lord, I will follow you *but* let me first go and bid them farewell who are at my house." Jesus rejects the condition in His response: "No one having put his hand to the plow and looking back is fit for the kingdom of God" (Luke 9:61–62). Most likely, Jesus goes on without him because he is unwilling to take a risk.

Keith Miller, in his book entitled *The Becomers,* helps us understand what Jesus means when He promises us, ". . . I will make you to become. . . ." Miller likens our spiritual development to the training of the trapeze artist.[1] The first step is to learn the skills of swinging on a single trapeze. When these skills are mastered, you are ready for the next lesson. Another trapeze is set to swinging in counterrhythm to the one you are on. It is time for a leap of faith! Risking your skills and security on the single trapeze, you leap into space at the precise moment to catch the second trapeze at the top of its swing. Learning and leaping, learning and leaping—that is the rhythm of risk-taking for the teachable disciples of Jesus Christ who are in the process of "becoming." With each leap comes learning that stretches our faith, increases our confidence and enlarges our ministry.

Three times in my career, God has asked me to leap
from the skills and security of one position to another. After
I had established my credentials as a scholar and professor
in the public university, I received an invitation to become
the president of a small, unaccredited, two-year Christian
college. My colleagues in higher education likened the move
to a professional ride "off into the sunset." Yet, as a minister
under mandate, and in counsel with my family, I leaped
and caught the swinging trapeze. After seven years as president of Spring Arbor College, the original goal of establishing a fully accredited, four-year Christian liberal arts
college had been achieved.

Rather than letting me enjoy the security of that new
status, the Lord set the trapeze of Seattle Pacific College
swinging into view. Even though it meant a transcontinental move for my young family away from our roots in Michigan and into an urban setting of a much larger institution
with a sizeable debt, we leaped. Fourteen years later, Seattle was our home, Seattle Pacific University was our love,
and to serve as president of the University until its centennial year of 1991 was our goal.

Then God started another trapeze swinging before me.
I was invited to take the presidency of Asbury Theological
Seminary. To accept the position meant another traumatic
transcontinental move for the family, a return to a rural
village, a step out of the national spotlight in higher education and an adjustment to the new field of graduate preparation in theology. With a mingling of faith and fear, I leaped
again. It is still too soon to get full perspective on this
latest change of career. Suffice it to say, God has confirmed
every promise He made to me when He asked me to take
the risk. My family and I would leap again.

Every leap of faith carries the risk of failure. Yet, ministers who suffer from "burnout, dropout or turnout" are
usually persons who will not take a risk. So often, ministers
who fail are those who have hung on to the security of
an old trapeze too long. Thus, they miss the exhilaration
of the leap, with its chance for failure as well as its prospect

for success and creative renewal. As Elizabeth O'Connor in her stimulating book, *The Eighth Day of Creation*, describes it,

> When we do not allow ourselves the possibility of failure . . . we are controlled by perfectionist strivings that inhibit the mysterious meshing of divergent lives within us. Spontaneity dies and the emergence of the unexpected ceases to be a possibility. We are literally tied and bound.[2]

If we take the risk, however, we open up the possibility of a creative breakthrough in our career and a spurt along the growth line of "becoming" a disciple of Jesus Christ. Previous studies of ministers have been preoccupied with the subject of burnout. It is time to study and extol the examples of clerical creativity where the qualities of spontaneity, humor, curiosity, imagination, enthusiasm, discrimination and persistence are alive and well in the life of the minister. To hazard a guess, such a study would show that the creative minister is a teachable person who is willing to take a risk. Jesus still calls for "becomers" who are open to learning, subject to discipline and willing to take a risk.

To Be Task-Oriented

At the same time that Jesus calls for disciples who are teachable, He does not summon those who are ever-learning and never-achieving. Fishermen are *task-oriented* people. When they go out in the morning, their survival depends upon their catch. Isaac Walton's adage, "God will not subtract from the allotted time of man the hours spent in fishing," does not apply to them. Simon and Andrew know fishing as a business, not a sport. To use a current cliché, they fish by the "bottom line." If their nets come up full, it is feast; if their nets come up empty, it is famine. Therefore, when Jesus calls them to be "fishers of men," they envision a task that requires them to accept responsibility for getting results by doing the right thing.

To be task-oriented is to get results. Effectiveness in ministry is a delicate balance between spiritual outcomes which are difficult to measure and practical results which must be measured. We have a natural reaction against evangelists who count souls like scalps and pastors who brag about buildings and budgets like holy hucksters. At the same time, we cannot excuse the evangelist or pastor who over-spiritualizes the ministerial task to defend the lack of results.

A superintendent sent me a copy of the centennial history of his conference. The leatherette binding and gold-leaf lettering represented the pride that he and his people had in their conference. Inside the book, however, statistics told another story. In 100 years more churches had been closed than opened and, on the average, only three new members were added to the church each year!

As fishermen who had to count their catch every day and as apostles who saw thousands added to the church day after day, Simon and Andrew would be baffled by this lack of results. In their ministry, spirituality and soul-winning were inseparable. Without denying their responsibility to be shepherds of the sheep, they could not forget their first calling to be fishers of men.

To be task-oriented is to be accountable. Results must be reported as well as achieved. Jesus calls Simon and Andrew to become "fishers of men" because it leaves no doubt about their responsibility to achieve results and be accountable. In the terms of management theory, Jesus gives them an RJP—a *realistic job preview.* His expectations for them are consistent with His own discipleship. Jesus takes the task that His Father gives Him to do, sees it through to the end and reports from the cross, "It is finished." Why, then, is the reporting of results resisted by so many ministers? Is it the idea that the minister is accountable only to God? Is it shrinking under the image of television preachers who count dollars and people in the millions? Is it a tendency to become so enamored with the process of ministry that the purpose and product are forgotten? Or is it another self-protective device against the lack of results? Jesus leaves no such ambiguity with the disciples when He calls them. To be "fishers of men" defines the task and sets the standard for measuring ministerial accountability. *To be task-oriented is to get the right things done.* Peter Drucker, the management expert, has a definition for effective leadership that is consistent with Jesus' standard for effective ministry. Drucker says that an effective leader is a person who pays more attention *to getting the* RIGHT THINGS DONE *than to getting* THINGS DONE RIGHT. [3] Notice what is right in Jesus' call for disciples who are accountable achievers. The emphasis is not upon statistics or structures, dollars or doctrines, theologies or things; it is upon *people.* If we are doing the right things in ministry, we are "fishers of men."

In recent years, leadership theory has done a flip-flop. After decades of developing rational theories of leadership, scholars are recognizing that great organizations are made by legendary leaders who focus a vision of human values which inspires, shapes and grows people. Even in the business of high technology, the successful companies are the ones whose leadership has brought the priority of people into focus. From their lesson, we ask a leading question, "Are we getting the *right things done* in our ministry?" If we are, our priority will be *people.*

On a Sunday morning forty years ago, a small black boy knelt in the sand of a side street playing marbles in Shreveport, Louisiana. The white minister of the local Free Methodist Church happened by and, on the spur of the moment, broke the code of the South and invited the boy to Sunday school. The black boy picked up his marbles and went to church. Soon, his family followed, creating a racial crisis in the town, the church and the denomination. Ten years later, with the aid of his church, the same black boy left the South to enroll at Spring Arbor Junior College in Michigan. As the only American black in the school, he was immediately dubbed "Jet" because of his color and his speed in the 100-yard dash.

After Jet had been in school for a year, our paths crossed. At the tender age of twenty-four and fresh out of seminary, I became his dean of men, sociology instructor and debate coach. Jet did not make my life easy. Just before I arrived, he had been party to a practical joke in the dormitory that led to tragedy. To initiate a new student who had the reputation for deep sleep and nightmares, the men in the hall got Jet to enter the room late at night, awaken the student with a gorilla's roar, and flash the whites of his eyes and teeth over his sleepy victim. When Jet played his part to perfection, the terrified student jumped through the second-floor window and broke both feet on the ground below. For months, there was fear that he would never walk again. Jet, of course, came close to dismissal, but finally escaped with rigid probation.

In sociology class, we encountered other issues. As a young professor, I saw my teaching on segregation in the South and discrimination in the North thoroughly tested with Jet sitting in the front row. He struggled, too. About that time, Jet became the target for a love-starved white girl. Hours of counseling went into the dilemma before we came to resolution. Out of our hours together, I invited Jet to join the debate team. As his coach, I had to start him at the most elementary level in verbal articulation, logical argument, case development and on-the-feet thinking for rebuttal. Still, in the championship tourney, Jet lost the debate because he failed to prepare his case for both sides of the question.

Thirty years passed. One night my wife and I attended the annual banquet of the Free Methodist Church in which the Layperson of the Year is honored. A distinguished black man came forward to be introduced as the Honorable Paul Lynch, the first black to be elected to a district court in Louisiana, leading layman of the Shreveport Free Methodist Church, trustee of Spring Arbor College, husband of a

Louisiana State professor, father of a gifted daughter and Democratic hopeful for the United States Congress. After a standing ovation, Judge Lynch responded extemporaneously—poised, articulate, logical, humble, humorous, spiritual—a master of the public platform.

Recalling his life history, the judge thanked God for the Free Methodist minister named Gilbert James, who dared to call him from the ring of marbles. Then his mind leaped forward to his days as a student at Spring Arbor Junior College. All of the weight of honors shifted when he said, "There I met a man named David McKenna. He taught me how to bring Christ into the issues of life."

Thirty years in the ministry of Christian higher education passed before my eyes. All of the earned degrees, innovative programs, balanced budgets, debt-free buildings and distinguished awards fell into order. There is no greater, higher or more satisfying reward for ministry than to be part of Christ's crew fishing for men. The "Jet" who became "Judge" is my proof.

The people whom we win, grow and bring to spiritual maturity not only provide the evidence that we are getting the right things done, but through their testimony our calling is relived and our ministry is renewed time and time again.

III

Reclaiming Our Promise

When Christ calls us to ministry, it is a mutual commitment. In His call, "Come follow me and I will make you become fishers of men," He asks us to be trustworthy, teachable and task-oriented. In turn, His call contains the promise that [He will be the *model* for our trust, *mentor* for our teaching and *manager* for our task.] This is a reciprocal relationship between the Caller and the Called that is unknown in the secular world and all too rare in the Christian world. On one side are the *expectations* that the pastor will be trustworthy, teachable and task-oriented. On the other side are the *resources* that Christ has personally promised to those whom He has called. As the model for our trust, He shows us the person that we can be. As the mentor for our teaching, He leads us into the truth we can know. As the manager for our task, He helps us be effective in what we do. Think what this means. Christ's investment in us is personal and total. He puts Himself on the line for our ministry! He is precommitted to our growth! He is pledged to our effectiveness! Therefore to reclaim His promise is to tap all the resources we need for the renewal of our ministry.

Reciprocal relationships between superiors and subordinates in formal organizations are usually defined by a contract. A person seeking employment will be presented with a task description that spells out the qualifications and the expectations for the job. In return for that investment of personal qualities and skills, the employer will specify the rewards of title, position and financial compensation. A contract is then prepared as a reciprocal agreement between the two parties—employer and employee. By definition the contract is functional, legal and impersonal. The employee provides the skills to perform a function in exchange for tangible rewards based upon performance. Little or nothing is said about the commitment of the employer to the human needs, the personal growth and the total well-being of the employee. Work under these circumstances can be dehumanizing and relationships between management and labor, as labor unions are witness, can be adversarial.

Jesus offers us a covenant, not a contract. In contrast to a contract that is functional, legal and impersonal, His covenant with us is relational, spiritual and personal. In the Old Testament God makes a covenant with the children of Israel that borders on contractual terms. If they obey His law, He will reward them with His blessing. The emphasis tends to be upon functional righteousness, legal justification and impersonal sacrifice. Jesus, however, fulfills God's intentions for the covenant by making it relational, spiritual and personal. Rather than a functional exchange of rewards for righteousness, Christ promises a relationship in which He invests Himself. In place of legal justification between the adversaries of a holy God and a sinful people, Christ gives us the free gift of grace which we do not merit and cannot earn. Instead of the impersonal production of the religious ritual, Christ promises us the experience of becoming personally whole and progressively well. Thus, to respond to the call to ministry is to enter into a covenant with Christ in which the exchange is uneven. His expectations are high but nothing compared to the resources that He provides in His relationship to us as the model for our trust, the mentor for our teaching and the manager for our tasks.

CHRIST OUR MODEL

In support of His call for us to be trustworthy, Jesus commits Himself to be our *model.* Although the disciples know the value of trust, they are human and subject to lapses. So in the company of Jesus for three-and-a-half years they witness unbroken trust in action. Jesus keeps every promise that He makes to them when He calls them.

Every minister needs a model. Fred Smith in his book *You and Your Network* draws a distinction between a hero and a model. A hero, he says, is a person who shows you who he can be. A model, on the other hand, is a person who shows you what you can do.[1] The distinction is probably academic. At an early age we might call our models heroes. Our heroes may be fictitious characters or eminent persons whom we do not know. I remember a *Life* magazine editorial many years ago in which Dag Hammarskjöld, Pope John XII and Albert Schweitzer were extolled as the heroes of the twentieth century. After reviewing their individual achievements, the article concluded with the statement that they shared one quality in common—because they chose to be good first, they became great later. Although I never met any of these three men, they became my heroes. I read every book that they wrote and most of the books written about them. They showed me the value of seeking first to be good rather than great.

Every minister needs a role model. Dr. James Gregory served as a president of Spring Arbor College when I was a freshman. In addition to his administrative duties, he taught Greek, homiletics and philosophy. Not only did I stand in awe of his towering intellect but I found myself thirsting for the Spirit of God which exuded from his teaching and his preaching. Perhaps he was too gentle and gracious to be a good administrator but when he disciplined me for a crude prank that I pulled in the residence hall, I felt as if I had betrayed his trust. When Dr. Gregory died he left me three personal items: his doctoral cap and gown, his leather-bound, gilt-edged copy of Thomas à Kempis's devotional classic *The Imitation of Christ* and his well-read edition of C. S. Lewis's autobiography, *Surprised by Joy.* Needless to say, I wore the gown when my doctorate was conferred, I keep *The Imitation of Christ* on my desk and I quote *Surprised by Joy* more often than any other book except the Bible. But even more important than the items are the values they communicated to me. Dr. Gregory left me the legacy of academic excellence, spiritual devotion and a joyful witness. In him I saw the spirit of Christ.

Our models then are persons who exemplify a quality of life to which we aspire. In human relationships, especially between leaders and followers, there is no higher value to be modeled than the quality of trust. Once trust is established and maintained under test, other values will follow. For this reason Jesus makes trust the quality of life that He will exemplify for His disciples.

Peter serves as our case in point. Immediately after the resurrection Jesus sends word for the disciples to meet Him in Galilee. In a phrase that should be immortalized as the evidence of a leader's commitment to His followers, the risen Lord says to the women in front of the empty tomb, "But go and tell His disciples *and Peter* that He is going before you into Galilee" (Mark 16:7). Although Peter betrayed the trust that Christ put in him, the Lord did not abandon His disciple. No wonder that the Epistles of Peter read like an autobiography of trust in the promises of God. Peter writes of Christ: "Leaving us an example, that you should follow in His steps: 'Who committed no sin, nor was guile found in His mouth' " (1 Peter 2:21–22).

Peter does not hesitate to recommend Jesus as a model to be followed. Imitation is the starting point of identification with our models. But we must go on. In the introduction to his Epistle, Peter reinforces our relationship to Jesus as the model for our trust with the strongest words of affirmation about the power of His person: "By which have been given to us exceedingly great and precious promises, that by these you may be partakers of the living nature; having escaped the corruption that is in the world through lust" (2 Peter 1:4).

As followers in His steps we imitate Christ; as "partakers of the divine nature" we personify Christ. Because He is the model of our trust, we can be trustworthy.

At each intersection of my ministerial career I have had to leave some person of my family or some part of my life in the hands of God. Each time He has given me a promise and asked me to trust Him. Needless to say, He has never gone back on His word. For every moment of desperation, doubt or despair my life history is an affirmation that God is utterly trustworthy. If only our past lessons of trust were transferable to the future, we would see ourselves daring to take bold steps with Him in our ministry. More important than that we would be able to say to others as the apostle Paul challenged the Corinthians, "Be . . . followers of me, even as I also am of Christ" (1 Cor. 11:1, KJV). Models need models.

CHRIST OUR MENTOR

Backing His call of us to be teachable, *Jesus promises to be our mentor.* As our model of trust, *Jesus shows us who we can be;* as our mentor for teaching, He leads us into *what we can know.* Leaders fail if they promise their followers a learning experience and do not teach them. Jesus sets a right example. Not only do His disciples become students in the large lecture and demonstration sessions of His ministry but they receive personal instruction in small groups and as individuals.

Mark Hopkins is a name in American higher education synonymous with master teaching. Educators say that the ideal teaching-learning experience is "Mark Hopkins on one end of the log and the student on the other." Logs may have been scarce in Jesus' time but He practices the principles of master teaching long before they were written into text books. His pledge to be the mentor for His disciples is so integral to Jesus' commitment that He promises them the Holy Spirit as their traveling tutor who will continue to teach them after He has gone to His Father.

A mentor, especially a spiritual mentor, is more than a master teacher. Yet all of the qualities of master teaching are evident in Jesus' method and style.

1. The expectations for learning are high, clear and consistent.
2. The relationship with a student is personal and humane.
3. The student is actively involved in the learning process.
4. The teacher's convictions are communicated with warmth and enthusiasm.

Certainly in Jesus' teaching relationship with His disciples, all of these qualities are present. One superlative dimension, however, stands out. Jesus is in special relationship, not only to the disciples as persons but to Truth, itself. As Parker Palmer writes in his book *To Know As We Are Known/A Spirituality of Education,*

> Jesus is a paradigm,
> a model of this personal truth.
> In Him, Truth, once understood
> as abstract, principled, propositional,
> suddenly takes on a human face and
> a human frame. In Jesus, the
> disembodied "Word" takes on flesh
> and walks among us.[2]

E. Stanley Jones identifies the uniqueness of Christianity
the same way when he notes that the "Word became flesh
and dwelt among us." In all other religions, Dr. Jones says,
the word remained the word. Learning from Jesus, then,
is a personal, spiritual and communal experience in which
the "Knower and Known" interrelate and interact in the
learning process.[3] Palmer chides Christian educators who
approach the truth as objective reality which is "out there"
as something to be observed and manipulated.[4] Pilate reveals this rationalistic perspective when he asks, "What
is truth?" By keeping truth as an external object, he can
avoid its impact upon his life and his responsibility to it.
Some modern scholars try the same tactic. Truth is viewed
as an ever-elusive object to be pursued, observed, manipulated and owned like a piece of real estate, but never acknowledged as absolute, assimilated as personal or
activated as transforming. Palmer's perception of truth refutes both Pilate's skepticism and the scholar's rationalism.
Truth is a word that derives from the Germanic root meaning "troth" as in the marriage vow " . . . and hereto I
pledge thee my troth." Thus,

> . . . with this word one person enters
> a covenant with another, a pledge
> to engage in a mutually accountable
> and transforming relationship, a
> relationship forged of trust and
> faith in the face of knowable
> risks.[5]

So behind Jesus' promise to be our mentor is His declaration, "I am the way, the Truth and the Life. No man comes
to the Father but by Me." His call to be teachable is an
invitation to enter into a relationship in which we are
pledged to Him who is the Truth and He is pledged to us
who can know the Truth. Our learning is personal, spiritual
and communal.

We see this relationship at work in the question that

the disciples asked of Jesus their mentor. Questions have a way of revealing the quality of the teaching-learning process. When the Scribes, Pharisees and Sadducees ask Jesus a question to trap Him, He counters with the biting edge of Truth. But when the disciples ask Jesus out of blundering ignorance, floundering faith or even selfish interests, He patiently responds with kingdom principles which are foundational for their faith. For instance, the disciples feel free to express their ignorance when they ask Jesus, "Why do you speak in parables?" Their mentor uses the question to inform them that they will know the mysteries of the kingdom because they have eyes to see and ears to hear while others do not. To illustrate His point, Jesus tells the parable of the sower, the seed and the different kinds of soil. Personally, spiritually and communally the disciples encounter Truth.

The acid test of Jesus' role as mentor to the disciples comes in questions of self-interest, such as when they ask, "Who then is the greatest in the kingdom of heaven?" (Matt. 18:1). Or in questions of theological confusion, such as "Who then can be saved?" (Matt. 19:25). And in questions of fear, such as Peter's inquiry on behalf of the Twelve, "See, we have left all and followed You. Therefore, what shall we have?" In each case, Jesus applies a principle of Truth which they can assimilate, practice and preach themselves.

Looking back upon my relationship with Dr. James Gregory, I realize that he served as my mentor as well as my model. He personified the Truth that he taught. Therefore, I not only gained valuable knowledge that I needed but I became pledged to the Truth of Jesus Christ that he so warmly taught and enthusiastically lived. A lifetime of learning and growing has followed because I became pledged to the Truth with him. Even though he is gone, the transfer is complete. Christ is my mentor and learning is a spiritual experience.

Just the other day, a former student who became a young

college president surprised me with a telephone call in which he said that he planned to resign his position. The greater surprise came, however, when he told of his lifelong dream to have me as his mentor. I realized then that mentors create mentors. As I had pledged myself to Truth in relationship to my mentor, Dr. Gregory, another person wanted to be pledged to Truth in relationship with me. Perhaps it is age but I also realized that my experiences, both joyous and painful, have given me a repertoire of knowledge and spirit that keeps me from repeating youthful errors and even gives me a perspective which my children occasionally call "wise." As with most students, I have not appreciated the discipline and stretching of what I have learned while in the heat of the learning process. But now I see the fidelity of Christ who calls me to be teachable. He through His Holy Spirit is my mentor and if I continue to be teachable there is no end to learning.

CHRIST OUR MANAGER

In support of His call for us to be task-oriented, Jesus commits Himself to be our *manager*. Few of us have the self-discipline to manage our own tasks. We need someone to help us set priorities, monitor our progress and evaluate our results. Clergy in particular need time and task management. We do not punch a clock, work a shift or report daily to a superior. In between the regular worship services and committee meetings, discretionary time is at a maximum. We choose our time for reading and writing, praying and speaking, counseling and calling. Without the management of priorities, Parkinson's Law takes over to fill up the available time with pressures of the moment. Of course, punctuating that discretionary time zone are crisis calls and urgent decisions. Jesus must have anticipated our needs when He committed Himself to be the manager of our tasks in ministry.

With the current emphasis upon visionary and charismatic leaders the role of the manager has fallen into some disrepute. Bennis and Nanus in their book *Leaders* follow the lead of Peter Drucker in suggesting that leaders get the right things done while managers get things done right. By inference, managers are plentiful but leaders are few. Presumably, managers are also more limited in people skills, more restricted in creative ideas and more narrow in breadth of perspective. An adage seems to evolve, "If you can't lead, manage."

In my opinion, managers deserve a better hearing. Without effective managers, leaders will fail. Visions must be implemented as well as articulated. In a recent meeting of a religious organization, a management consultant went through the steps of articulating the vision, setting the goals, planning the strategy and devising the tactics for the board of directors. In the middle of his talk one of the executives in the organization passed a note to me on which was written, "This is just what you told us six years ago. The missing step is *implementation.*" As persons who are responsible for implementing the vision of leaders, no apology needs to be made for the role of the manager. Management is a gift to be cultivated and honored.

Each of us needs management help in three areas of our work: (1) allocation of scarce resources; (2) access to vital information; and (3) skill in making critical task decisions.[6] Jesus served as the manager for the disciples in each of these areas. When He sent them out two-by-two He gave them the instruction to shake the dust off their feet and move on from places where the gospel was rejected. At first His order seems cruel and contradictory to a God of love and patience. But we must remember the limitations of time, space and energy with which the disciples had to deal. Their purpose was to proclaim the gospel as widely as possible. Human tendencies would cause them to persist in preaching the gospel in the same place until it was accepted. Jesus, their manager, tells them to move on.

Vital information is the key to power among individuals and within corporations. Both superiors and subordinates will control and manipulate information to build and preserve their power base. On the other hand vital information can be managed to build confidence in subordinates and achieve long-term goals.

In Luke 9:20–21 Peter answers Jesus' question, "But who do you say that I am?" with the inspired confession, "The God and Christ." Jesus responds strangely. He strictly warns the disciples and commands them to tell no one. Why does He want to withhold this vital information from the public? Jesus takes the disciples into His confidence by informing them for the first time that He must suffer and die. In management, timing is essential for sharing vital information. If the information is released too early, a larger purpose can be aborted. If the information is released too late, a bad decision can be made. In this case Jesus manages the vital information about His deity in order to avoid a premature confrontation with His enemies before He has had the time to complete the preparation of His disciples.

The management of our ministry is particularly needed when we are called upon to make critical task decisions. Almost daily a pastor encounters issues and problems for which there are no immediate precedents or obvious solutions. Every energy of mind and spirit must be engaged in the process of critical thinking, spiritual discernment, sound judgment and compassionate concern. The quality of these critical task decisions determines the effectiveness of our ministry. Yet more often than not we must admit that we do not have the wisdom or the foresight to make the decisions on our own. We can, however, claim the promise of Christ that He will be the manager for our critical tasks.

While Jesus was on the Mount of Transfiguration with Peter, James and John, His other disciples encountered a violent demonic spirit in a boy whose father had brought him to them for healing. They faced a critical task decision and failed. Afterward, they asked Jesus, "Why could we not cast him out?" His answer tells us how He brings the resources we need to our critical task, "This kind can come out by nothing except prayer and fasting" (Mark 9:29). The power of prayer and the discipline of fasting combine as the management principle for the working of miracles.

Jesus' promise to be the manager of the disciples' critical task continues after the resurrection. Just before His ascension, He leaves them a commission that involves a specific strategy for world evangelism. Then, with the coming of the Holy Spirit, He guides them in tactical decisions to increase the effectiveness of their ministry. The Acts of the Apostles reads like a manager's manual for "fishers of men."

The promise of Christ is still good. Through the Holy Spirit we have the resources for the management of our ministry, especially for our critical tasks. Although we all want to think that we are capable of self-management, the fact is that we flounder when we try to do God's work without the management of His Holy Spirit.

There is a grand purpose in Christ's promise to be the model for our trust, the mentor of our teaching and the manager for our tasks. His most astonishing words are: "Most assuredly, I say to you, he who believes in Me, the works that I do he will do also; *and greater works than these he will do,* because I go to My Father" (John 14:12, italics mine).

This promise is utterly incomprehensible and totally unbelievable without the resources that Christ has promised to us. With His resources, however, every pastor can post the promise on the wall of his study for all to see:

AND GREATER WORKS THAN THESE WILL YOU DO

To relive our calling is to hear Christ beckon us once again, "Come after Me and I will make you fishers of men." To reconfirm our commitment is to give ourselves to Him as trustworthy friends, teachable disciples and task-oriented co-workers. To renew our ministry is to tap again the resources He has provided for us as our model for trusting, our mentor for teaching and our manager for achieving. Will we respond? Mark invokes his favorite word when he reports that Simon and Andrew *"immediately* left their nets"* to follow Jesus. When James and John heard the same call, they *"immediately* left their father"* and got into step. Jesus still expects a quick and clean decision. Therefore, to rekindle our romance with ministry and restore our dream for ministry, we need to respond to Christ's call and repeat our vows:

> A charge to keep I have
> A God to glorify
> A never-dying soul to save
> And fit it for the sky.
>
> IMMEDIATELY!

IV

Respecting Our Differences

During my senior year in college I served as pastor of a small-town church. The gadfly of the church took one look at me and my nineteen-year-old bride on our first pastoral call and exclaimed, "Why, you ain't even dry behind the ears yet!" Nevertheless, we were a welcome relief to the pastor who had been asked to leave the church as a ministerial failure. He persisted, however, in pursuing his calling by changing denominations and taking a three-point charge in the northern woods. Six months later I chanced to meet his district superintendent at a ministerial conference. When he found out where I pastored and whom I followed, he exclaimed, "Tell your bishop that if he has any more failures like Harry, send them my way. He is doing an outstanding job for us."

How can we account for such a radical turnaround in pastoral effectiveness? To begin with, we need to realize that a perfect pastor is hard to find. Whether we are clergy or laity, we expect a charismatic personality, a biblical authority, an aggressive evangelist, a confident teacher, an able administrator, a compassionate counselor, a community leader and a denominational statesman—all in the same person. To paraphrase an already apocryphal story, the elders of a Baptist church nursed similar expectations when they were searching for a pastor. After the qualities of the ideal minister were spelled out, a search committee went to work. Futility followed their efforts because no one measured up to their requirements. Finally, after months of searching, an elder called a special meeting of the committee to announce, "Stop the search. I have found our pastor. His credentials are impeccable. He is unsurpassed in spirituality, intelligence, human relations, preaching and administration. There is only one question about him. Is God a Baptist?"

Once the demand for perfection is eliminated, the beauty of individual differences in the diversity of ministry of gifts can be appreciated. Each pastor brings unique qualities to the call of God. Howard Snyder, in *The Community of the King,* illustrates how the Spirit of God works with our individuality by using the analogy of a glass prism.[1] The countless crystals of the prism represent the variations of personalities, gifts and experiences that members bring to the body of Christ. The intense light of God's Spirit shines into the prism, refracts within it and reflects out on the other side a spectrum of spiritual gifts that are as varied as the colors of the rainbow. We accept that analogy for our laity, why not for our pastors? We, too, vary through an infinite spectrum of personalities, gifts and styles that are reflections of the light of the Spirit of God shining through us.

HONORING OUR DIFFERENCES

Just before Richard Nixon's downfall, James David Barbour published *The Presidential Character* as a study of chief executive styles.[2] To provide a framework for his study, Barbour set up a two-dimensional chart. On the vertical axis, the president was rated from active to passive in performance and horizontally from positive to negative in attitude. Thus, four presidential styles were identified in the quarters marked off by the intersecting lines: active-positive, active-negative, passive-positive and passive-negative.

John Kennedy was described as an active-positive president—a program-centered leader who used his charismatic personality to focus a lofty vision in innovative programs. Without doubt, Kennedy relished his brief stay in Camelot, even though comics dubbed the administration he shared with his brother Bobby as the "grim world of the brothers wonderful."

Richard Nixon served as an example of an active-negative president—a power-conscious leader who does a lot but has little fun. Despite Watergate, Nixon will be recognized by history as a strong leader, even though his public image will still be flawed by a jutting jowl and vulgar language.

Barbour is not quite sure, but I would characterize Dwight Eisenhower as a passive-positive president—a person-centered executive with minimal achievements but lots of image and affection. No other president in recent times has had the power of an infectious smile which evoked the good feeling behind the chant that won him the presidency, "I like Ike."

The fourth leadership style is represented by Calvin Coolidge—a passive-negative president whose administration centered upon propriety as a civic virtue and counted upon duty as a substitute for political rough-and-tumble. Although Coolidge left little that is "worthy to history," he did give us the key to his presidential style when he said, "Let men in presidential office substitute the light that comes from the midnight oil for the limelight."

Do pastors have similar leadership styles? To borrow from Barbour's study, we can visualize the following framework for studying pastors.

LEADERSHIP STYLE

	Positive	Negative
Active	active-positive leader (program)	active-negative leader (person)
Passive	passive-positive leader (power)	passive-negative leader (propriety)

Think about an *active-positive* pastor. He or she is a task-centered achiever who thoroughly enjoys the clerical role. Aggressive programs are proposed for the church, such as faith-pledges for capital projects and risk commitments for evangelistic ventures. Preaching, too, is active-positive. Sermons—whether topical, textual or expository—expound a vision and frequently translate into pep talks for Christian involvement in the life of the church. Results often follow. Heads are numbered, spaces measured, dollars are counted and successes are touted. An active-positive pastor is an achiever who has fun in ministry. The criticism of being a superstar with superficial results may apply. As with John F. Kennedy, serious historians are asking, "What did he really do?" Yet the aura remains with memories of days when we were all caught up in the vision of Camelot. Our "Pastor Jack" might well conclude his inaugural sermon with the same heart-tugging plea, "Ask not what your church can do for you, but what you can do for your church."

Power rather than program motivates the *active-negative* pastor. Vigorous action is still the theme of the ministerial leader but the grace notes are missing. Tight control is exercised over the life of the church, and the pastor's office (and the power-center) is the Sunday morning pulpit. Decentralized ministries such as self-initiated lay evangelism and semi-independent Bible study and prayer groups are tolerated but not encouraged. Not unexpectedly an active-negative pastor lives with tension and moves from crisis to crisis. Who decides whether the next building will be a chapel or an educational unit? What is the role of the personnel committee and the influence of the new youth pastor? Why can't church members give part of their time and tithe to other evangelical ministries? Yet once the decisions are made and the pastor's authority is confirmed, strong and effective leadership follows. An active-negative pastor might entitle his ministerial memoirs *My Six Crises,* and if you caught him on the down cycle when his authority was being questioned, his farewell address to the sermon might conclude with the words, "You won't have this pastor to kick around any more."

A *passive-positive* leader with a person-centered ministry may seem to be the most desirable ministerial style, but it is not necessarily the most effective. Little is done but everyone feels warm and stroked. Consequently, even the noble discontent out of which new ideas develop may upset the equilibrium of the status quo in which a passive-positive attitude thrives. Heavy stress is put upon an organic or interpersonal model of the church as superior to achievement or authority. Sermons glow with the relational theology of individual potential and corporate community. One can almost see the passive-positive minister in the pulpit, a shining face that exudes trust and outstretched arms topped by a "V" sign at the fingertips. The congregation chants, "We like our pastor Ike."

Duty characterizes a *passive-negative* style of ministerial leadership. Achievements are limited, imagination is missing and the personality is dull—but stability is guaranteed. A passive-negative leader is a textbook minister who daily checks off the chores of his work. Whether making pastoral calls or planning programs, there is a faint rustle of pages from the manual on church administration. Not surprisingly, a passive-negative attitude threads through the pastor's sermons with such themes as Christian consistency, influence and responsibility. Church members who vary from these dutiful virtues remain enigmas to their all-work-and-no-play pastor. If asked to sum up his view of the ministry, a passive-negative pastor might even echo Coolidge himself, "Let men in pastoral office substitute the light that comes from the midnight oil for the limelight."

DEPLOYING OUR GIFTS

Labels of good, better or best cannot be pasted over these differences in pastoral personalities. The division of pastoral styles into four categories is convenient only for understanding some working premises for deploying our gifts in ministry while preserving our individuality. Our first working principle is that *effective pastors cannot be stereotyped by personality.* If we were asked to rate the four pastoral styles for success, we would undoubtedly give preference to the active-positive personality and work downward. In doing so, we would rule out some of Jesus' disciples, many apostles and most saints. The truth is that we have been victimized by a secular standard of success. Pastoral styles are put on a vertical scale with the active-positive personality at the top and all other styles rated as inferior in quality and secondary in success. Pastors who do not fit the stereotype may try to emulate the ideal or succumb to the perception that they are mediocre.

A secular standard for pastoral success is an insult to God. He calls passive-negative as well as active-positive persons into His ministry. Contrary to some expectations, God does not try to change the personalities of the persons whom He calls. Conversion reverses our direction, justification cancels our sin, regeneration transforms our lives and sanctification sets us apart for service—but only to make the most of the personality we have inherited and learned. A duty-centered sinner is not likely to become a bombastic saint. Neither is an authoritative achiever apt to become known as a soft-spoken and easy-going pastoral spirit.

There are exceptions, but most often God honors the uniqueness of our personalities by drawing out our gifts rather than reworking His creation or rewriting our life history. Imagine how boring the Bible would be if it were written only by active-positive authors. The same truth applies to ministry. Only with the full range of personality and style can the Holy Spirit orchestrate the differences and lead a symphony.

In the book *Leaders* by Warren Bennis and Burton Nanus, four strategies for leadership are identified in a tell-tale chapter entitled, "Leading Others, Managing Yourself."[3] Strategy 4 is *the deployment of self through positive self-regard.* The principle applies to pastors of all personality types and leadership styles. Positive self-regard can be achieved or enhanced by

   . . . recognizing our strengths and compensating
       for weaknesses
   . . . nurturing our skills with discipline
       and
   . . . discerning the fit between our
       perceived skills and what the job requires.

Once again, secular prophets have spoken to biblical truth. Rather than succumbing to a singular model of leadership, they remind us that it is the deployment of the individual self through positive self-regard that characterizes effective leadership. In biblical terms, positive self-regard is recognizing, discipling and nurturing our gifts in order to deploy ourselves in servanthood.

It is time to tip the ladder of ministerial success from a vertical to a horizontal position. On the horizontal plane the infinite variety of pastoral personalities and styles are recognized for their individual work and potential for effective ministry. With the ladder laid flat we can also turn our attention from climbing to growing. A pastoral growth plan for professional, personal and spiritual development can be readily designed on the three-to-five-year schedule with periodic evaluation of progress toward the mutually agreed-upon goals. Even without the formal instrument, however, every pastor can implement the threefold plan for developing positive self-regard: (1) knowing our strengths, (2) nurturing our skills and (3) discerning the fit between our gifts and the needs of our ministry. Once we are working this plan, we can deploy ourselves and begin to see the results of our servanthood, namely, the evidence of positive self-regard building in our people which in turn leads to their self-deployment or servanthood. It all begins with recognizing the worth of every pastoral personality and the potential of every pastoral style.

A second working principle is to realize that *churches have personalities too*. Although endless studies have been done on church organization and management, little has been done on the culture of the individual church. Yet everyone knows that churches have personalities which might well fit into the same categories as active-positive, active-negative, passive-positive and passive-negative pastoral styles. Again for the sake of simplicity, churches might be sorted out by determining whether the weight of emphasis is given to program, people, power or propriety. Whatever the emphasis, the culture of churches can persist just as persons persevere in personality. Each of us has experienced fits and misfits with churches we have attended, visited or pastored. In fact, one study of churches showed that parishioners drove miles through the city and passed other churches of the same denomination to attend the church of their choice, or more appropriately, compatibility. The issue is being aggravated by people who are bringing a consumer mentality to their choice of churches. Denomination, theology, preaching, behavior standards and even spirituality can become secondary to personal compatibility with the culture of the church.

Culture is more than the formal declaration and the official organization of a church. To know the personality of the church, you must understand the informal flow of power, the hierarchy of value, the nuances of ethnocentricity, the families of reputation, the tradition held sacred, the hidden expectations and the prevailing tone in the

congregation. The old joke about the unlearned elder of
the church who opposed the installation of chandeliers because as he said, "They are too expensive, no one can play
them and sooner or later we are going to need lights," is
closer to the truth than we realize.

One pastor failed in a church because he refused to wear
a robe on Sunday morning, another one succeeded because
he did not fight the ethnic loyalists who demanded that
the gymnasium be painted in the colors of their native
land and still another failed when he tried to bring a biblical
curriculum into Sunday school classes which had developed
as closed generational groups who drank coffee and caught
up with the news for thirty to forty minutes of the Sunday
school hour. On and on we could go, citing the successes
and failures of pastors who encountered the persistent personality of the local church.

Once again, we must confront the reality that successful
churches are placed on a vertical scale with the active-
positive personality as the epitome. My heart sinks whenever I receive a brochure on a workshop for pastors based
upon a model of a highly visible and successful church.
While there are valuable lessons we could learn from each
other, it is an error to assume that the settings, styles and
strategy of one church can be transferred to another church
without being customized for the situation.

Out of a genuine desire to build the church, we grasp
for new emphases in theology and new methods of evangelism as panaceas for success. Yet, in an unpublished survey
of *Leadership* magazine readers, the pastors reported their
frustration at coming home from conferences, seminars and
workshops with surefire ideas for renewing and even revolu-
tionizing their churches. When they enthusiastically presented their dreams to the laity of the church, however,
neither the fire of their enthusiasm nor the drama of their
dreams could be transferred.

Is it possible that the resulting frustration is the symptom
of a personality conflict not so much between the pastor

and the laity as between his plans and the personality of
the church? For instance, to propose active-positive plans
for immediate adoption by a passive-negative church is to
invite disaster. Therefore, to preserve the integrity of the
church's personality, the laity will either summarily reject
the plans or devise defense mechanisms against their fulfillment. Churches, like individuals, have a thousand ways
to protect their personality.

Thoughts about the personality differences of pastors and
churches lead us naturally to the next working principle:
*the match between the personality of the pastor and the
church is situational.* If persistence rules the personalities
of pastors and churches, then care must be taken to make
their match compatible. Perhaps in idealizing the pastoral
role and standardizing the church culture, we have tended
to assume that any pastor can succeed in any church at
any time. More often, however, pastor-church appoint-
ments and invitations are made with the hope for construc-
tive change on the part of one or both parties. Not enough
attention is paid to the circumstances that can help us
predict the fulfillment, frustration or failure of the expectations for both pastor and church.

A long-term beloved pastor retired from a strong, growing
church in a university town. The congregation embarked
on a national search for his replacement and by a unani-
mous vote brought a well-known evangelical leader to the
church as pastor. The honeymoon lasted only six months
before the pastor and the elders faced off in a confrontation
over pastoral goals and style. When the heated discussion
got down to the nub of the issue the standoff between personalities became evident. The pastor brought with him
a glamorous reputation as an active-positive builder of aggressive and innovative church programs. His predecessor,
however, had been a passive-positive personality, focusing
upon people and letting the elders develop the policy and
run the programs.

The problem, then, started shortly after the new pastor's

arrival. He began to spell out his vision for the church from the pulpit and announce his plans in committee meetings. Who would dare argue with success? Professors from the university formed the core for leadership among the elders. They brought to their role the "collegial" structure of the university in which professors expect to be involved as peers in the creation of policy, plans and programs for the institution. Information from the inside revealed that the pastor's programs were needed and workable but they failed because he missed the timing and neglected the process. In other words, he failed to read the personality of the church. The elders also shared responsibility because they wanted another passive-positive pastor who focused on people while they held the power for policy, planning and programs.

Similar instances involving a variety of factors can be recited endlessly in the biographies of pastors and the histories of churches. While there is no hard-and-fast rule for matching the personalities of pastors and churches, one thing is clear: pastoral styles and church cultures tend to persist and if the expectations are in conflict the relationship is doomed unless one or both parties change.

Our fourth working principle follows: *pastoral styles and church cultures change slowly, by circumstances as well as by design.* Some sage once said of colleges, "It takes twenty-five years for a college to win a reputation and twenty-five years to lose a reputation." The same may be said for churches. There may be change but it is always slow. In his retirement sermon, after twenty-two years in the same pulpit, a minister friend said, "I have outlived my critics." He brought change to the church, not by changing people but by cultivating a new generation.

Sometimes social change will solve a problem and create new problems in a church. Twenty years ago I attended a church that became known as the graveyard of pastors. Relocation, advertising, door-to-door evangelism, church growth programs, city-wide campaigns, Christian radio—

nothing made the difference. A second suburban relocation seemed equally futile. Then, the last of the old generation died. Another new pastor came and, most importantly, the suburbs moved to the church. Yesterday's church of a hundred is now today's church of a thousand. Facilities are overrun and a third relocation with a sanctuary for 2,000 is being planned. Partially by social accident which became part of providential design, the personality of the church has changed. Time and circumstances, however, cannot be ignored. More often than not, if a church changes its personality, it is because the pastor and the congregation catch the timely tide of social change rather than create a revolution.

Still, every pastor in every situation becomes what Bennis and Nanus call a "social architect" shaping the future of the church. Whatever the pastoral style—emphasizing program, people, power or propriety—a compelling vision for the future of the church needs to be seen, communicated and implemented by the leadership of the church. Whether the people march forward together by following their leader or by developing that vision with him is incidental to the values of creating an effective church and preserving the pastoral personality.

In his first letter to the Corinthians, Paul recognizes different pastoral leadership styles. He writes,

> Now there are diversities of gifts,
>   but the same Spirit;
> There are differences of ministries,
>   but the same Lord.
> And there are diversities of activities
>   but it is the same God who works all in all.
>   (1 Cor. 12:4–6)

Without textual violation could we now also write, "And there are variations in pastoral style—some active-positive, some active-negative, some passive-positive and some passive-negative—but it is the same God who works all in all"?

God honors our differences when He calls us to ministry and expects us to use our knowledge and His wisdom to deploy those differences to meet specific needs in a context of positive self-regard. In God's good will for pastors, personalities are preserved, differences are affirmed and diverse needs are met. We must never forget, a pastor is a many-splendored person.

V

Regaining Our Balance

My first model for the ministry was a barnstorming preacher who thundered from the pulpit, "Bless God, I would rather burn out than rust out." Guilt stalked me for years. Unless I was obsessively engaged in nonstop preaching that was leading onward and upward to the glory of early breakdown or death, I was cheating on my calling. A Sunday out of the pulpit twitted my conscience, a happy vacation stabbed at my soul and any thought of change from the preaching ministry was condemned as the ultimate betrayal. Even good health provoked the question, "Am I doing my best for the kingdom of God?" If I wasn't burning out, I must be rusting out.

Who would have thought that pastoral burnout has now become an occupational hazard for the ministry? Today it is so popular that it has replaced the ulcer as the sure sign of success. Of course, we all deny that we are victims. I remember my defense when a director of nursing for a university hospital watched me fiddle with silverware and shred a paper napkin during a dinner with friends. She riveted her eyes on me and announced, "You are a classic type A personality—a prime target for a heart attack." Immediately I went out to buy the book *Type A Behavior and Your Heart* by Friedman and Rosenman.[1] I never got to the symptoms of my Type A personality because I took seriously the research design from which the authors built their descriptions of Type A and Type B behaviors. In their search for a sample in the San Francisco Bay area, they quickly identified goal-oriented, time-urgent, napkin-shredding executives with a high risk of heart disease. But they could not find eighty Type B personalities in that metropolis of millions until they reached the level and sampled the professions of clerks in municipal government and embalmers in funeral parlors! Then and there I chose my future with the hurrying, hostile, happy, aggressive, anxious and achieving types known as "A."

Still there is a time for slowing down and smelling the flowers. A first-grader wanted some attention from his father who had brought home an attaché case filled with letters to answer and reports to write. Mother tried to explain, "Daddy is a very important and busy man. He cannot get all of his work done at the office during the day." Familiar images spun in the first-grader's mind and the question came back, "Then why doesn't the teacher put him in a slower group?"

As an indispensable step toward the renewal of our ministry, we must join a slower group and think about regaining our balance. Of necessity, we must begin with the subject of "pastoral burnout" as a symptom of a ministry out of balance.

Pastoral Burnout

Studies of pastoral burnout have produced a plethora of books on the subject. They range from Freudenberger's psychiatric study *Burnout: The High Cost of High Achievement*[2] to the books that focus specifically on the

pastoral ministry, including Rediger's *Coping with Clergy
Burnout*[3] and Donald Demaray's *Watch Out for Burnout.*[4]

To save you from reading all of these books, let me state
the findings that I consider most essential for understanding "pastoral burnout." *First, persons who are burning out
share common symptoms, but those who are building up
show rich variation in personal qualities.* Burnout symptoms are always the same even though their intensity may
vary in individuals. They include:

> . . . exhaustion
> . . . cynicism
> . . . irritability
> . . . withdrawal
> . . . sleeplessness
> . . . anxiety
> . . . noncommunication
> and
> . . . loss of humor.

Among these symptoms, two stand out. *If we are exhausted at the end of the day and cannot sleep at night,
the warning light of burnout is glowing red.*

In contrast there is rich and uncommon variation in the
lives of people who are being renewed and "building up."
People who are positively well and becoming progressively
whole are:

> . . . energetic
> . . . optimistic
> . . . calm
> . . . open
> . . . creative
> . . . competent
> . . . communicative
> and
> . . . laughing!

As you can see, each of these qualities for building up
has the potential for continuing growth, creative combina-
tions and infinite expression.

A second and corollary finding of burnout studies is that being well is more than the absence of the symptoms of being sick. Bruce Larson has written a book with a lengthy title, *There's a Lot More to Health Than Not Being Sick.*[5] Simply said, *being well is not the opposite of being sick and building up is not the opposite of burning out.* Wholistic medicine is developed along a continuum that begins at one end with a *cure* of disease, moves to the middle ground in the *prevention* of symptoms and advances toward the other end, which is *wellness* or *wholeness* of the physical, emotional and spiritual being. Our goal is more than the cure of the disease or the prevention of the symptoms of pastoral burnout; it is to build up pastors as persons who are positively well and becoming progressively whole.

A disturbing question enters our thoughts at this point. *Why are people in the helping professions, especially the clergy, so susceptible to burnout?* A study by Jerry Edelwich suggests that the problem begins with the idealistic expectations of ministerial students.[6] Once in the pastorate, however, their idealism collides with their reality of limited resources, excessive public demand and inadequate criteria for measuring pastoral performance. Disillusionment follows after five to seven years in the ministry. At that time, either the person has changed, the church changes pastors—or the pastor burns out.

Idealistic expectations may be a major cause for "burnout" in the ministry. But keep in mind the continuum that moves from curing the disease through prevention of symptoms to the building of wellness and wholeness. Reducing the level of pastoral expectations is only a coping mechanism for dealing with symptoms. God's Word shows us His desire for building pastors who are positively well and becoming progressively whole.

THE ELIJAH SYNDROME

Sooner or later every study of pastoral burnout illustrates the problem by what is called "The Elijah Syndrome." The

saga of Elijah's ascendancy as the prominent prophet of
God is recorded in 1 Kings 17–19. Called to his prophetic
profession in a time of famine and civil war, Elijah was
fed by ravens, a widow saw him work miracles, kings
quaked at his name, God answered his prayer by fire and
false prophets died by his hand. Yet on the signal from
Jezebel that she will revenge the death of the prophets
of Baal before the sun goes down on another day, Elijah
panics and plummets into the aggravated symptoms of
prophetic or pastoral burnout.

Elijah is not a victim of idealistic expectations. He does
not reach too high; he accomplishes too much. His triumph
over the prophets of Baal on Mount Carmel qualifies as a
"peak experience" in which God takes him far beyond his
own expectations. Elijah expects the fire of God to consume
only the sacrifice, but God overwhelms him as well as the
false prophets when the tongue of flame licks up the wood
and stone of the altar, and even the water flowing through
the trenches! Under the power of the same Spirit, Elijah
exercises the faith that sees a cloud the size of a man's
hand on the horizon with the promise of rain on the parched
land. Under the same energy of the Spirit, he outruns
Ahab's chariot in a fifteen-mile mini-marathon over the
hills and dales between Mt. Carmel and Jezreel.

How then do we account for Elijah's flame-out? Like the
altar on Mt. Carmel, he becomes just a charred shell of
his original self—exhausted, withdrawn, paranoid and
wanting to die. Specialists in burnout will be quick to identify *prolonged and excessive stress* as the cause of Elijah's
despair. Stress can be creative or destructive. Creative
stress is highly individualized. Bill Russell, one of the greatest centers in basketball, says that unless he threw up in
the locker room before every big game, he knew that he
was not ready to play. In contrast, Fred Taylor, the coach
of Jerry Lucas at Ohio State, said that he knew Jerry was
ready to play his best when he saw him gently rubbing
his thumb along the tips of his fingers during warm-ups.
Stress is destructive when it is excessive and prolonged.

Elijah has carried the weight of the nation and the destiny of the kingdom upon his shoulders during a time of prolonged crisis. He doesn't eat, he doesn't pray, he doesn't rest, he doesn't play—he only speaks the Word of God and performs miracles. His problem comes because he tries to do it all by himself. More often than not, the fueling factor for a flame-out is not our idealistic expectations, but our individualistic achievement. Off a peak experience, we fall victim to "the Elijah Syndrome."

Isolation is the earliest symptom of "the Elijah Syndrome." We withdraw from our role, our setting, our family and our friends. Like Elijah, we flee either literally or symbolically into the wilderness, leaving our servant behind in Beersheba (1 Kings 19:3). Isolation is a coping mechanism for pastors who work hard for lofty goals in high-stress situations. Its partner is *escapism*. How many pastors suffer from "cinematic neurosis"? It is the late-night escape into old movies and television reruns. Whatever the outlet, escapism is an early sign of burnout.

Once isolated and alone, Elijah sits under a broom tree asking to die. *Depression* is a progressive symptom of pastoral burnout. Freudenberger says, "Despair is the letdown that comes in between crises or directly after 'mission accomplished.' "[7] He compares Elijah's despair to postpartum depression that a woman knows after the birth of a baby. The symptoms are the same: ". . . sadness, separation, sluggishness, and above all, emptiness."[8] Leaders are particularly susceptible to these symptoms. Lincoln, whom we extol as the greatest of our presidents, spoke about the "black dog of depression" that pursued his soul. Georgia Harkness describes the despair of saints of all ages in her book *The Dark Night of the Soul.*[9]

Total exhaustion is the companion for Elijah's isolation and depression. He who has displayed the energy to outrun Ahab's chariot now falls into exhausted sleep, awakening only for the angel's food, and then back to sleep again. All of us know that our bodies need only so much sleep for physical restoration. Beyond that time, excessive sleep is a symptom of depression, not fatigue. D. G. Kehl, writing in *Christianity Today,* suggests that candidates for exhaustion are leaders who are cursed with the role and the power that gives them a "sense of omnipotence."[10] Elijah suffered under that curse. Ravens served him, widows marveled at him, kings called him "lord," masses fell on their faces before him, false prophets cowered at his feet—and even the clouds confirmed his faith.

Pastors are subject to the same curse. People obey our orders, show us deference, give us discounts, second-guess our desires, hang on to our words, and flatter us until we are convinced that we can outrun chariots—or walk on water! Sooner or later, we have to return from that ego trip, and when we do, exhaustion may be the consequence. We need to take the advice of crusty old Harry Truman who said, "If a president begins to believe that the band is playing 'Hail to the Chief' for him, he is in trouble. It is for the office of the presidency, not the man."

After deep sleep begins to "knit up the raveled sleeve of care" for Elijah, he gains enough presence of mind to re-open communication with God. Does the conversation sound familiar? Elijah reminds God of his unselfish, unstinting service as a prophet and projects his bitterness upon the people who do not appreciate him or what he does for them. His own words trigger the jaws of a fatal trap. In self-pity, Elijah moans, "I, even I only, am left." The prophet has come to believe that he is *indispensable.*

A change of pastorates is like a change of presidencies. It is at least a temporary cure for feelings of indispensability. Having served three presidencies, I know whereof I speak. Students at Spring Arbor College do not recognize me from the artist's drawing on the portrait wall of presidents. I can even walk through McKenna Hall on the Seattle Pacific University campus and remain anonymous. Why then do I continue to carry the burden of indispensability into my current presidency at Asbury Theological Seminary? I feel guilty being away from the campus; I feel guilty staying on the campus. I do other people's work and fret because no one works as hard, as fast, or as effectively as I do.

Both presidents and pastors need people to care about them, and most of us are surrounded by these people. I am. But if we think that we are indispensable, we will never feel adequately appreciated. In fact, the "Elijah Syndrome" bottoms out when the prophet becomes paranoid. Elijah complains to God, "They seek my life, to take it away." If Elijah were alive today, he would drive a car with a bumper sticker that reads, "I'd be O.K. if you paranoids would quit following me." It is a short step from feeling unappreciated to feeling persecuted.

The "Elijah Syndrome," then, gives us a different view of pastoral burnout. His expectations are not unrealistic, his stress is not beyond control and boredom is the least of his problems. Still, he falls in flames with the symptoms to which a successful pastor is particularly susceptible—feeling isolated, depressed, exhausted and indispensable.

Now that we have our patient thoroughly dissected, a footnote is in order. I find myself reacting against all of the attention we give to burnout as another one of those self-improvement problems involving self-analysis, self-development and self-esteem. Introspection has become an exercise that is an end in itself. To regain our perspective in anticipation of seeing how God renews Elijah, I turn to Erma Bombeck's best-selling devotional companion entitled *Aunt Erma's Cope Book,* subtitled "How to Get from Monday to Friday . . . in Twelve Days." As a spoof on all the stuff about self-improvement, Erma makes some pithy and theologically sound vows. Never again does she want to see the words, "input," "concept," "feedback" or "bottom line." Never again does she want to hear the words, "share with you" or "at this point in my life." Then, in a postscript, she concludes with this gem,

In her infinite wisdom, my mother offered me yet another observation after my months of self-examination, devotion to improvement, and quest for happiness. She said, "I'll be glad when you hit menopause. It'll take your mind off your problems."[11]

BACK TO BALANCE

God has to get Elijah's mind off his problems. In a series of encounters, He turns the attention of the prophet from self-pity to renewed strength when an angel shakes Elijah out of his depressive sleep with a command, *"Get up and eat."* More often than not, the process of pastoral renewal begins with physical conditioning. Our annual Ministers' Conference at Asbury Theological Seminary is impoverished by the fact that we do not have a seminar on physical exercise for pastors taught by Dr. J. C. McPheeters, our esteemed second president, who died in 1983 at the age of 94. He knew the secret that bounced him out of bed every morning with the shout on his lips, "This is the day that the Lord hath made. Let us rejoice and be glad in it." Who else could waterski twenty miles on his ninety-second birthday! Dr. McPheeters knew the biblical truth that is being confirmed every day by wholistic medicine— body, mind and spirit are one. The interrelationship is astounding. Pioneer research by David Moberg and others is showing spiritual values as one of the most significant factors in motivating changes in lifestyle to promote health. A study at Johns Hopkins goes so far as to reveal a positive correlation between weekly church attendance and the reduction of hypertension, increased longevity and resistance to infection.

Sad to say, there is still separation between Christian theology and practice in responding to the unity of persons. Institutionally we program the separation and individually we prove it. Still, biblical wholeness begins with self-awareness of the systemic nature of body, mind and spirit. "Get in touch with your body before your body gets in touch with you" is the first word that the burned-out pastor will

hear from a physician. Angels fed Elijah to restore his physical strength as the starting point for renewing his mind
and refreshing his spirit. We are responsible for our own
bodies. Hard facts tell us that our parishioners think of
health as the absence of physical symptoms, not as the
potential for wellness and wholeness. Concern is not lack-
ing, but understanding is. Therefore, it is sound advice to
recommend to pastors, "Get in touch with your body before
it gets in touch with you." Your physical, mental and spiritual health depends on it.

On the strength of angel food, Elijah travels forty days
and forty nights until he reaches Horeb, the mountain of
God. But still in a state of fear and flight, he finds a cave
and spends the night there. In the morning the Lord comes
and asks him, "What are you doing here, Elijah?" The answer is classic for a burned-out prophet: "I have worked
very hard for the Lord God of the heavens; but the people
of Israel have broken their covenant with you and torn
down your altars and killed your prophets, and only I
am left; and now they are trying to kill me too" (1 Kings
19:10, TLB).

God is very patient. Instead of squashing a prophet who
has become a pouting paranoid, He gives him the second
command for recovery: "*Go out, and stand on the mountain*
before the Lord. And behold the Lord passed by" (1 Kings
19:11).

Caves are places where we see no farther than the walls
around us and, according to Plato's *Allegory of the Cave*,
we mistake the shadows for reality. A mountain, however,
is a sure cure for a sense of omnipotence and a feeling of
being indispensable. Dwarfed by the panoramic scene that
stretches up, out and around us, we regain the perspective
of our prophetic calling.

On the mountain top Elijah is invited into the presence
of God, not by wind, earthquake or fire, but by a still, small
voice. In every study of pastoral burnout there is the pre-
scription for "healing silence." Physiological research

shows that a period of silence reduces every physical symptom of stress while smoothing out the brain-waves so that the mind is opened to reflection, perspective and creativity required for the big picture. When James Dobson was asked how he accounts for the spectacular surge in his ministry to the family, his answer is that his ministry began to grow when he put priority on his devotional life.

Out of the "healing silence" in the presence of God, Elijah regains the balance for his ministry. Holistic medicine is based on the axiom that every illness or symptom of burnout is caused by an imbalance in the person—whether physical, psychological or spiritual. Elijah suffers from the imbalance of work. In the flurry of defending the faith, he loses the rhythm of life. Work, rest, worship and play are the keynotes of life that need rhythm. While differing in priority, time and position in our lives, they must be in balance and none can be neglected.

Wayne Oates has a perfectly delightful book entitled *Workaholics, Make Laziness Work for You.* He prescribes doses of "creative laziness for healthy living." Minimal doses are mildly therapeutic and maximal doses of laziness are lethal. In between are the moderate doses of laziness that give life its "flavor, character and strength." Among the punchy recommendations in Oates's survival kit for lazy people are:

> Always have a perfect excuse for everything.
> Your schedule has become overgrown, mow it!
> Dare to let things happen.
> Do it now, loaf later.
> Stay down for the count of nine
> and
> Let the rats win the rat race.[12]

When was the last time you disappeared and dared to remain incommunicado? Oates gives me justification for the disappearing act I learned from a university president many years ago. Every Tuesday afternoon my calendar reads "seminar." If someone calls, my secretary says, "I am sorry, the president is in a seminar and cannot be disturbed." Only death, disaster or development calls can keep me from my weekly tennis match. Like the "runner's high" that only we joggers know, it takes a mountain top to see the "big picture" once again.

From the mountaintop Elijah also sees the Lord passing by. One of the advantages in representing the seminary on the national and international scene is the opportunity to see the panorama of the Lord's parade. To a recent meeting, we invited Jerry Falwell and James Wallis, two persons who are worlds apart. In our minds, at least, Falwell represents the far right and James Wallis the far left of evangelical social action. In that meeting, Jerry Falwell spoke with pride about his role in electing Ronald Reagan to the presidency by registering two million people in churches across the country. James Wallis, on the other hand, declared that Reagan's election was the darkest day in American history for the poor of the nation. Yet as they talked in separate interviews, each of them spoke of their first love as pastors and their single desire to show the spirit of Christ in their dealings. So when we asked them about their "growing edge" for future ministry, Jerry Falwell spoke enthusiastically about 100 or more centers for ministering to unwed mothers who choose not to have an abortion. Jim Wallis' eyes gleamed as he talked about planning a revival in his church. Even though I may not agree completely with either of their positions or tactics, I left the meeting humbled by the knowledge that the Spirit of God was at work, maturing and balancing their ministries. Out of the cave and on the mountaintop for just a moment, I saw the Lord passing by.

Elijah is still not ready for what he sees. Winds, quakes and fire literally tear the earth apart, but the Lord is not in them. Then, after the fire, the Lord comes in a "gentle whisper" (1 Kings 19:12, NIV). Elijah pulls his cloak over his face and heads back for the cave. Before he gets in the Lord asks again, "What are you doing here, Elijah?"

The prophet repeats his pitiful plaint: "I have been very zealous for the Lord God of hosts; because the children of Israel have forsaken Your covenant, torn down Your altars, and killed your prophets with the sword. I alone am left, and they seek to take my life."

Thus, God's third command for Elijah is, *"Go back the way you came . . . ."* Further instructions included the responsibility for anointing Hazael, king of Aram, Jehu, king of Israel, and Elisha, his sucessor as a prophet. Then, with just the edge of holy sarcasm, the Lord says, in a free translation: "Incidentally, there are 7,000 men in Israel whose knees have not bowed to Baal and whose mouth have not kissed him."

In response to Elijah's withdrawal from human relationships that produced the sad cry, "I, alone, am left," God restores his network of human relationships. At the center of the network is his relationship with his *friend,* Elisha, who will also become his successor. Related to the center is the *functional* relationship to the kings whom he will anoint. In the larger relationship then, there is the *fraternal* relationship with 7,000 men who remained true to God. We need all three—friend, functional and fraternal relationships—as the life-support system for our ministry. Pines and Aronson in their book entitled *Burnout: From Tedium to Personal Growth,* deal with the problem of people in the helping professions being exhausted by the constant scrutiny and demand of the public, known as the "fishbowl effect."[13] To prevent or cure burnout, a well-defined social support system of enduring interpersonal relationships is essential. Family, friends and colleagues are needed to:

> . . . listen to us
> . . . appreciate us
> . . . challenge us
> . . . support us
>   and
> . . . test us.

A wife, husband and family are closest to the center of the circle, especially for listening, emotional support and reality testing. Shortly after my first inauguration as a college president, my seven-year-old son asked the question, "Daddy, is President Kennedy great?" "Yes," I answered, "he is a great president." Hesitating for just a moment, my son came to the heart of the matter, "Well, you're a president. Why aren't you great?" While we need spouses and children to love and humble us, other friends are needed for professional support and professional challenge. Paradoxically, we have to define the boundaries of our human relationships to expand the breadth of our ministry. Elijah has to relearn how to relate to people as the cure for trying to do it all alone.

Recently I visited with my friend William Turner, a prominent Christian leader in his business, community and church in Columbus, Georgia. Each time I visit Bill, I come away inspired by some new evidence of his spiritual insight and growth. Last spring we conferred upon him an honorary degree in recognition of his role as a lay leader in the United Methodist Church. When I asked Bill what he would say in one sentence to seminary graduates who are about to begin their pastoral ministry, he answered quick as a wink, "I would put this sign on the wall of their study: *Remember, God has other workers.*"

The way to recovery from pastoral burnout is simple and clear:

> *Get up and eat . . .*—to refresh our body, mind and spirit.
>
> *Go up and stand on the mountain . . .*—to re-enter His presence and regain our perspective of God at work.
>
> *Go back the way you came . . .*—to restore our prophetic role and our personal relationships.

Therapy for burnout always begins by going back a step at a time and changing our daily habits. Just before my father died at an early age of a massive heart attack, he sent me a handwritten copy of Cardinal Richard Cushing's prayer, "Slow Me Down, Lord." Perhaps in premonition of his own death, he thought that his son needed to slow down. Maybe we all do as a first step in going back the way we came.

> Slow me down, Lord. Ease the pounding of my heart by the quieting of my mind. Steady my hurried pace with the vision of the eternal reach of time. Give me, amid the confusion of the day, the calmness of the everlasting hills. Break the tensions of my nerves and muscles with the soothing music of the singing streams that live in my memory. Help me to know the magical restoring power of sleep. Teach me the art of taking minute vacations; of slowing down to look at a flower, to chat with a friend, to pat a dog, to read a good book. Remind me each day of the fable of the hare and the tortoise, that I may know that the race is not always to the swift, that there is more to life than its increasing speed. Let me look upward into the branches of the towering oak, and know that it grew great and strong because it grew slowly and well. Slow me down, Lord, and inspire me to send my roots deep into the soil of life's enduring values that I may grow toward the stars of my greater destiny.

And all pastors who want to be positively well and to be progressively whole will say, *"Amen."*

VI

Recycling Our Resources

Golden parachutes are not provided for pastors who bail out of ministry. In the corporate world, talented executives who rise to the top on the average last only four or five years as president of the company. During this time, every creative resource is tapped to the point of exhaustion. Then, if not "bumped up" to be chairman of the board or set aside as a "floating apex" with a paper title, the president is forced to bail out of the organization, but always on a "golden parachute" of financial security that eases the fall to earth. The gilded parachute is the compensation for the total investment and often the utter exhaustion of human resources required of leadership in the corporate structure.

A pastor who is forced to bail out of ministry is given no golden parachute. The fall is precipitous, the "thud" is resounding—and the aftermath is devastating. Not only does a pastor suffer the downfall of identity but finds no cushion of financial security with which to ease the impact of the sudden stop. Yet our attitude toward the human resources that a pastor invests in ministry is not unlike the secular view of the corporate community. We assume that a pastor is a person who is expended for the church and expendable in ministry. If we believed otherwise, we would have a plan for conserving the precious resources of pastoral leadership and preventing the forced bail-out from ministry due to exhaustion. The answer is not a golden parachute, but biblical stewardship for the human resources that we expect pastors to invest in ministry.

A Principle for Pastoral Renewal

Few of us would subscribe to the view that a worn-out pastor is the best pastor. Yet, in practice, we are slow to change that attitude. For instance, *pastoral leadership is assumed to be an unlimited resource.* If a pastor dies, breaks down, drops out or betrays the sacred trust, our grief is short because we assume that God always has others waiting in the wings. Such an assumption is only half true. Certainly God will get His work done, but never at the expense of His creation. Equally certain is the fact that He has a special concern for those whom He has called and anointed to be His ministerial servants. Pastoral leadership is not an unlimited commodity to be used up and thrown away; it is a scarce and precious resource to be conserved, renewed and expanded.

One half-truth leads to another. Conservationists warn us about "straight-line" or "linear" thinking that results from the presumption that our natural resources are unlimited. The gas crisis of 1977 is an example. Americans presumed that an unlimited oil supply could be charted on a solid, straight line rising onward and upward into infinity. Our gas-guzzling "balloon" was punctured first by The Club of Rome report informing us that the oil supply was not unlimited. In fact, the end of the line could be seen. The second shock came when the line was redrawn as a falling rather than a rising line—and the third shock came when the Arabs cut the line in mid-course. Yet, even today, most Americans do not believe that the oil supply is limited and running out. Even if we did, we rest in the easy confidence that our technology can save us or our military might can guarantee whatever fuel we need.

Straight-line thinking about pastoral leadership has similarities when applied to the ministerial career. Once a minister is called, it is assumed that God backs up the call with unlimited resources to go on forever, rising at all times on an unbroken line of activity. If the line is cut short, temporarily interrupted or reversed from rising to falling, something is wrong with the minister—not in the way in which we use and develop our resources.

Waste and pollution are companions to the straight-line thinking that natural resources are unlimited. Kenneth Boulding describes our throwaway world with the phrase, "A cowboy economy." Picture a cowboy riding across the desert, blazing a trail with the ashes, bones and garbage of his campfires. Sometimes the ministerial profession looks like a desert over which a cowboy has ridden and moved on, leaving the debris of burned-out pastors on the trail behind. A critic of the church once said, "It is the only army that shoots its wounded." Broken-down, burned-out and cast-off pastors blaze the trail of the ministry. By the scores they sit on the sidelines in our churches, sell real estate for a livelihood and counsel in the public schools as an option. If only they could be renewed rather than rejected, there would be no shortage of pastors.

Bad attitudes have gotten us into our fix; biblical attitudes will deliver us. To begin with, *we must put a premium upon pastoral leadership as a scarce rather than an unlimited resource.* Good pastors are hard to find and we cannot afford to lose one of them. Likewise, the call of God to preach is a special gift that cannot be treated lightly or taken as common. God's grief for one of His chosen servants

who drops out, breaks down or fails must become our grief
and God's glowing hope for the young and gifted minister
must become our hope. We will then be taking a steward's
responsibility for recycling our pastors.

Experts in the field of recycling physical resources will
be quick to spot the fallacy in the idea of recycling pastors.
Whenever physical resources such as wood, metal, gas, oil
or coal are recycled, the quality of the product drops with
each successive cycle. School children know that the Law
of Entropy is at work. According to this law, the universe
is running down and its physical resources deteriorate with
use. A recycled piece of wood never has the quality of the
original log.

If the Law of Entropy alone is applied to recycling pastors, we would only be able to conserve their physical energies—but never stop the inevitable march to exhaustion
and death. This is where a Law of Biblical Dynamics takes
over. It is the Law of Syntropy which states that spiritual
and intellectual resources improve and expand with use
and re-use. How else could Paul have written, "Beloved,
now are we the sons of God and it does not yet appear
what we shall be"?

So, two counterforces are at work in the universe, each
bearing upon the recycling of pastors. One is the Law of
Entropy that applies to the physical energies of the pastor;
the other is the Law of Syntropy that applies to the spiritual
and intellectual resources the person brings to the ministry.

Without falling into the platonic trap of separating flesh
and spirit, we know that God will restore the quality of
the spiritual universe when He fashions a new heaven and
a new earth. On the way to that day, we are obligated to
conserve His physical resources and use them wisely. Our
responsibility for spiritual resources is just the opposite.
We are to exploit with reckless abandon our spiritual and
intellectual resources because they enlarge in scope and
gain in quality when used and re-used. To return to Boulding's "cowboy economy," imagine the desert blooming as

a rose with the beauty of expanding and improving spiritual resources that are being used fully time and again.

Carry the picture of the desert in bloom into a plan for recycling pastors. Admittedly, ministers have physical bodies which age and die so that the principles of energy conservation must be applied, but they also have spiritual and intellectual resources which expand and become enriched with use and age. Recycling pastors, then, is a balance of the two principles. Physical resources are to be conserved; spiritual and intellectual resources are to be exploited. In combination, these principles will change our attitudes toward pastoral leadership and commit us to a plan for pastoral development.

A PLAN FOR PASTORAL DEVELOPMENT

As another telltale indicator of our wasteful attitude toward pastoral leadership, *most churches make no provision for the care and feeding of the minister.* Pastors are expected to care for others, but who cares for the pastor? A pastor is a person who works in a fishbowl on twenty-four-hour call at minimum pay and without job security. Any other professional would organize a union or a protective society and hire a lobbyist to promote higher wages, improved benefits and better working conditions. Pastors do not think or act this way. Instead, they give, they serve and they sacrifice—usually without verbal complaint. Maybe that is why churches tend to let their pastors go on until there are visible signs of fatigue or failure. Then, sympathy rises and Band-Aids are applied. Too late. The crisis could have been avoided by charging someone with the responsibility for preventive pastoral care.

Churches are not alone in neglecting their leadership. During the past twenty years as a college president, I have served as a director on several kinds of boards—religious, educational and civic—at local, state and national levels. Even though these boards are peopled by the top leadership of churches, colleges and corporations, they have two faults in common. One is the failure to provide adequate orientation for new board members. It is assumed that every new director understands the organization with all of the nuances of its historical development, interpersonal dynamics and interlocking policies. Most board members waste a three-year term warming up. The other fault is the failure to provide a personal and professional growth plan for executive development. Great care is taken in the selection process for executive leadership, but once the appointment is made, the board says by inference, "Now you're on your own." As a sign of confidence, it is good; but more often than not, it also shows a lack of care. The image of the tough-minded, self-made, goal-oriented executive carries over from board to board with a "dog-eat-dog, make-it-or-break-it" attitude. Consequently, I have accepted the personal mission to make trustee orientation and executive development my particular contribution to the boards on which I serve. Neither comes easily.

Recently, I completed a three-year, non-renewable term on the board of a national educational association. My final act was to chair the nominating committee. We recommended the re-election of the president of the association on the condition that the chairman of the board confer personally with the president about his plans and needs and that the board itself evaluate his performance in executive session. When I reported for the nominating committee, I was surprised by the cavalier approach to the recommendation. As usual, time was at a premium, so no executive session was held and no chairman's report was given. The president was re-elected unanimously without discussion.

The next day, the new board met with one-third new members. A continuing member chose the occasion to draw-and-quarter the president of the association who had been re-elected a few hours earlier. New board members were baffled by the attack and wondered what kind of responsibility they had accepted. The lesson should have been learned the night before. If a board member had reason to question the performance of the president of the association, it should have been voiced in executive session before the new board took over. Also, the retiring chairman should have reported on his evaluation of the plans and needs of the executive. To risk a pun, both went by the board. After the attack upon the executive, no one dared talk about his developmental needs as a person or as a professional. Most likely, his days are numbered.

Churches can correct these monumental errors by assigning either a standing or a special committee with the responsibility for pastoral development. The chairman of the group should be a person who understands leadership, genuinely cares for the pastor and has the confidence of the church. Whoever that person may be, he or she has the responsibility to sit down with the pastor, share frustrations as well as aspirations and plan out a future for growing and changing ministerial leadership. Later on, that same person must be able to objectify an evaluation of the pastor which may range from praise for a job well done to a recommendation for pastoral change. At all times, however, priority must be given to the good of the church and the growth of the pastor.

The specific task of the committee charged with pastoral development is to prepare and individualize a long-range plan for pastoral growth and renewal. Churches can take a cue from the academic community. During the days when American higher education was bursting with student and campus growth, faculty members were upwardly mobile. No longer. With the decline of the student population, the stunting of campus growth, the oversupply of Ph.D.'s in many fields and the impact of inflationary costs, the teaching community suddenly finds itself immobilized. The result is frustration that cannot be vented by a change of position. Turning inward, the faculties of the 1980s are predicted to organize unions, resist administrative leadership and suffer through a long period of low morale.

Campus leaders who have anticipated these realities have

turned their attention to faculty development. It is the only way to improve the quality of teaching when upward mobility is blocked and the number of young teachers entering the field is severely limited. So, deans sit down with faculty members to develop individualized and long-term growth and renewal plans. Goals are set—not just for the improvement of teaching within the institution, but also for such aspirations of the professor as scholarship, writing, consulting and community service.

Higher education is being forced to recognize the faculty as a natural resource that cannot be thrown away. Churches should come to that same viewpoint—not as a tool in a survival kit, but as a truth of Christian stewardship. To begin, the plan should project the personal and professional goals of the pastor. Personal goals might include physical fitness, family relationships, economic planning, avocational interests, travel and friendships. When I interview a candidate for a position, I find that questions along these lines reveal more about the person than the standardized questions on the professional evaluation sheet.

Of course, the personalized aspects of a pastoral development plan are not a substitute for specific professional targets. A minister will probably identify his professional goals with a vision of the church, but that is not enough. The pastoral role has many functions and no pastor excels at all of them. Therefore, there will be priorities which build upon a pastor's strengths and others that correct obvious weaknesses.

One pastor may envision a period when primary attention will be given to developing an expository pulpit; another may foresee the long-range need for a small group ministry to nurture new converts; and still another may recognize the need for a thrust into the community. Priorities will depend upon pacing. Neither a pastor nor a church runs at the same pace all the time. There are spurts of growth followed by pauses for consolidating the gains. A pastor must learn to read the pace of the church and respond with a matching ministry.

Almost without exception, a far-sighted professional development plan will include some advance, in-service education focusing upon intellectual development for the pastor. One look at the changes in the seminary curriculum during the past ten years is convincing proof that today's ministers cannot serve effectively during the next ten years without upgrading pastoral theory and practice. A church that wants to grow and be renewed with its pastor will include the opportunity for in-service education as an ongoing commitment to professional development.

No pastoral development plan would be complete without a forward look to spiritual growth and development according to the Law of Syntropy. Specific goals may be harder to define, but the question must be asked, "What are your spiritual goals as a person and as a pastor during the next three to five years?" Whenever I ask this question of a candidate, the person responds with surprise, "No one has ever asked me that before." But their surprise does not stymie them. After a moment's reflection when they seem to be reaching deep into the center of their being, they will give such answers as, "I want to learn to be more compassionate." "I need to learn patience." "I want to be a person of prayer." "I want to be a student of the Word of God." Contrary to our hidden and unrealistic expectations, ministers are not mature with all the fruits of the Spirit. Every one of them has spiritual needs and aspirations that should be identified—not to exploit their weaknesses, but to provide for their growth. In the context of a pastoral development plan, spiritual aspirations give flattering recognition to the fact that the pastor is fully human.

Recycling the physical resources of the pastor is a matter of time. Some pastors can work effectively over long periods of time without breaks because they have the enviable capacity to work when they work and play when they play. Most of us get tired because we do not leave the work behind

when we play and the play behind when we work. Indefatig-
able people do not mix the two. Like a Bjorn Borg on the
tennis court, they excel in work or play and have superhu-
man energy for prolonged and strenuous tasks because
nothing can break their power of concentration. Pastors
would do well to cultivate a power of concentration that
leaves church problems at home when they head for the
golf course and forget wishful dreams about birdie putts
when they close the door of their pastoral study.

Other pastors have learned the secret of personal and
spiritual recycling by taking five-minute vacations. A five-
minute nap at the office or a five-minute walk restores the
energy for another long stint on the job. I am a five-minute
vacationer. Often I have just one hour at home between
the end of an office day and an evening appointment.
Stretched out prone on the sofa with the evening paper
as a tent over my chest, I am instantly asleep and awaken
five minutes later with a surge of energy that can take
me through another four or five hours of work.

Other people are quite different. I know a high-energy
pastor who charges through an eighty-hour week, but needs
one day of isolation in his camper for physical and spiritual
renewal. Still another friend works for six months without
a break until the coiled spring of physical energy unwinds
and spiritual nerves are frayed. At that time, the only re-
course is a total break from the scene for two or three
weeks. After the semiannual break, he returns with fresh
energy for another six-month marathon.

Vacations must be individualized. Many pastors try to
piece together their vacation schedule a day or two at a
time. For most of us, a vacation by bits and pieces only
whets the appetite for relaxation. An old saw says that it
takes the first three days of vacation for a busy executive
to make the transition from work to play. Whether or not
that is true for every individual is a matter of debate, but
the principle is sound. It takes a block of uninterrupted
time for the body to renew itself and for the mind to gain

perspective. For me, vacations move through three stages—relaxation, renewal and readiness to return to work. The length of time needed to complete the cycle depends upon the physical and mental condition with which I began the vacation. More and more, I concur with corporations that require employees to take their full vacations annually—and with the friend who believes that vacations should be taken in large blocks of time, if not all at once. There is also a case to be made for increasing vacation time with age. One doctor has recommended that vacation time match a person's age with three weeks in the 30s, four weeks in the 40s, five weeks in the 50s and six weeks in the 60s. He must have had in mind the recycling principle that physical resources run down with use and age and therefore need more time for renewal.

A Proposal for Pastoral Sabbaticals

Vacations are primarily for the conservation of physical resources. *Sabbatical time is needed for spiritual and intellectual growth.* A sabbatical break after seven years of work is a biblical concept related to the Year of Jubilee. Preaching on the subject, however, is usually limited to sabbaticals for the soil and freedom for the slaves. Until recent years, only the academic community picked up the concept by granting sabbatical time to professors after seven years of teaching. Now, sabbaticals are being extended to academic administrators and corporate executives. They, too, need renewal after seven years in a pressure cooker.

Sabbaticals should also be introduced for pastors. They qualify by the personal and professional expectations that we place upon them. Few would debate a pastor's need for physical renewal after seven years of intensive public ministry. The greater need, however, is for a block of time for spiritual and intellectual renewal. Even though a pastor conscientiously reads and studies each week for sermon preparation, the multiple demands of the ministry restrict study in depth, limit the exploration of new ideas and work against experimentation with new programs. The purpose of a sabbatical is to provide an unencumbered block of time when the pastor can renew mind and spirit by pursuing an idea or a project on the growing edge of the ministry. I can imagine a pastor fulfilling a lifelong dream to study at a great university, write a long-delayed book, serve on the mission field or in the ghetto, or intern under the tutelage of a renowned minister.

If the committee on pastoral development follows the policies of the academic community, the pastoral development plan will provide a sabbatical of three to six months after five to seven years of service. When a sabbatical is earned, the pastor presents a proposal for the sabbatical project. If approved, the committee then takes responsibility to provide the resources required to free the pastor and sustain the church during the sabbatical period. In turn, the pastor accepts the obligation to prepare a formal report to the committee, and demonstrate the value of the experience in continuing service to the congregation. A sabbatical is a biblically sound investment in the growth potential of pastoral leadership as a scarce and valued natural resource of the church.

A Prospectus for Pastoral Growth and Change

A pastoral development plan includes evaluation. For some reason, professionals in every field resist evaluation. Doctors assume that no one can judge their performance except their peers in the profession, unless criminal activity is involved. Professors also assume that only their colleagues can evaluate their performance, except when there is legal proof of insanity, immorality or incompetence. These strongholds are falling. Doctors and professors are becoming vulnerable to malpractice suits. In the days ahead, objective and regular evaluation of the professions—

either from within or without—must be expected.

Pastors are equally resistant to evaluation. The typical argument is that spiritual outcomes cannot be measured by numbers. I agree, but not if it means that the pastor is evaluated by default. Without a formal evaluation, based upon specific expectations and performance standards, pastors tend to be evaluated by hidden expectations and personality quirks. Perhaps that is why pastors succumb to evaluation by numbers—members, converts, budgets and buildings. At least, the standards are objective.

A pastoral development plan should fit in between the extremes of unmeasurable goals and comparative numbers. When the pastor prepares a long-term plan for personal, professional and spiritual growth, goals are being set. If the committee on pastoral development accepts that plan, it also accepts the goals against which the performance of the pastor is to be measured. These goals must be kept in focus for both continuing and periodic evaluation. Otherwise, judgments about pastoral performance slip into hidden expectations, personality differences and head counts.

A formal evaluation of pastoral growth and change should be planned on a three-to-five-year cycle. It is an educational experience for the whole congregation to be involved, assuming that they have also been informed of the goals for the church and the pastor. The results of the evaluation should lead into the next cycle of pastoral growth and change. If the goals have been achieved, two alternatives are open. One is to project forward the goals for the next cycle of the church and the pastor. Assuming that these goals are compatible, a mutual commitment should be made to restart the cycle. If they are not compatible with either church needs or pastoral aspirations, a change for the pastor should be considered, not as proof of failure, but as an opportunity for continuing growth.

Of course, if the goals of the church and the pastor have

not been met, the critical question "Why?" must be asked in order to propose adjustments that may be as modest as a restatement of goals or as radical as a change of ministers. Contrary to thinking in ruts, the best pastor may be the one who grows out of a job and chooses to change pastorates. A person who is gifted in church planting, for instance, should be honored, not condemned, for following his gifts and moving on to plant another church. According to the viewpoint of waste and pollution, that minister should adapt to all of the seasons of church change and growth; but according to the recycling viewpoint of leadership resources, the same pastor would move to a new opportunity with dignity. I suspect that the ego of the church is at stake, even more than the pastor's. If pastors could move with honor after they have maximized their gifts in a given situation, they would welcome the change. Evaluation of pastoral performance must include all these options.

During the past year, I have observed the work of a search committee seeking a senior pastor for a church. A well-documented survey of the church and its needs produced some shocking results. An aging university church in a transitional urban setting proved to be both a threat and a challenge. Some candidates ran for cover and others did not qualify. Finally, with a clear sense of God's leading, the church called a person whose potential matched the challenge. Now what? The search committee has self-destructed, the congregation is relieved and the pastor is on his own. Except for the grace of God, all of the forces for leadership waste and pollution are in motion. If only a committee on pastoral development could be charged with the responsibility to develop the potential of a gifted pastor, the church and the pastor would change and grow together. I ask, "What is our obligation to the conservation of his physical energies and the expansion of his spiritual and intellectual potential?" Unless we have a pastoral development plan geared to these goals and a committee charged with the responsibility to see it through, he will be subject to the whims of individuals and changing circumstances. If only we could see him as a scarce and valuable resource to be physically conserved and spritually expanded, his future and the future of the church would both be enhanced.

The recycling of pastors is a biblical move for a daring church.

VII

Remembering Our Servanthood

Of all the professions, a pastor lives with the greatest tension between being a servant and a leader. Jesus poses a dilemma for us when He says, "Whosoever will be great among you, let him be your minister, and whosoever will be chief among you, let him be your servant" (Matt. 20:26, 27, KJV). On one side of the paradox is our image of a leader—a person with power, charisma and success. Trouble begins when we try to reconcile that image with our thoughts about a servant—submissive, self-effacing and unsung. Try as we might, human efforts to combine these qualities into the role of the servant-leader fail us.

E. F. Shumacher, in his book *Good Work*, expresses our frustration in two conflicting images of leadership. One image is the shining star at the top of the Christmas tree—bright, visible and dominant. The other image is the balloon-seller at the country fair—a drab and paltry holder of strings.[1] In human terms, one is a leader; the other is a servant. Only a cryptic mind can see through the fallacy in both images. The shining star at the top of the Christmas tree depends upon nuts in the branches, while the holder of strings depends upon hot air in the balloons above! Needless to say, the paradox of the servant-leader can be resolved only in the example given to us by Jesus Christ Himself.

A case study in Scripture illustrates the Spirit of Jesus Christ as we see servant-leaders, clergy and laity, in action. In the opening chapters of the Acts of the Apostles, we read about the miraculous growth of the church after Pentecost. Then it happens! Numbers of converts outrun the available food supply, internal conflict develops and the infant church is threatened with early extinction. Acts 6:1–6 records the conflict and the resolution:

> Now in those days, when the number of the disciples was multiplying, there arose a murmuring against the Hebrews by the Hellenists, because their widows were neglected in the daily distribution. Then the twelve summoned the multitude of the disciples and said, "It is not desirable that we should leave the word of God and serve tables. Therefore, brethren, seek out from among you seven men of good reputation, full of the Holy Spirit and wisdom, whom we may appoint over this business; but we will give ourselves continually to prayer and to the ministry of the word." And the saying pleased the whole multitude. And they chose Stephen, a man full of faith and the Holy Spirit, and Philip, Prochorus, Nicanor, Timon, Parmenas, and Nicolas, a Proselyte from Antioch, whom they set before the apostles; and when they had prayed, they laid hands on them.

The outline for analyzing our case for servant-leadership comes directly from the text. *To lead is to serve*

> . . . in human conflict
> . . . by personal example
> . . . with redemptive results

SERVING IN HUMAN CONFLICT

Conflict is the climate in which leaders rise and serve. Whether ancient or contemporary, local or international, secular or sacred, the ingredients of conflict are the same. First, *when the demand for limited resources outruns the supply,* we have the fuel for conflict. In our case study, either the needs or the wants of the Grecian widows outran the food supply. They claimed that they were not getting their fair share. In microcosm, this is the source of conflict through human history. World wars have been fought for domination of the limited resources of land and sea. Future wars will be fought over the distribution of the exhaustible resources of oil and the restricted resources of grain. Perhaps even now the only thing that keeps us from holocaust is the virtually unlimited, or at least unexplored, resources under the sea and out in space, or as the scientists put it, "The ocean's bottom and the moon's behind." Still, no prophetic revelation is needed to forecast the continuation of human conflict over the allocation of resources, not just the physical resources of *time, space, money, food* and *energy,* but the human resources of *people,* the political resources of *power,* the intellectual resources of *ideas* and the theological resources of *doctrine.* Whether in a secular or spiritual setting, whenever resources are limited and demand outruns the supply, human conflict is a possibility.

A second ingredient that ignites the fuel of conflict is what happens when *people divide into factions and begin to act out of self-interest.* Legitimate roles in any organization can become contentious factions. In our case study we see that two or three days before the crisis in the early church, the whole body of believers was united in heart and soul (see Acts 4:32). How quickly the unity disappears, not because food runs short, but because factions of self-interest take over. Greeks line up against Jews to complain about discrimination in the distribution of food. Like the racism that surfaced in Chicago's election for mayor in

1983, latent ethnic hostilities between the Greeks and the Hebrews fired the conflict. Under the unity of the Spirit they had buried the hatchet, but the handle remained close to the surface.

All organizations carry the potential for conflict in the legitimate roles that can become factions of self-interest— employer and employees, administration and staff, bishops and superintendents, clergy and laity. Whenever these legitimate roles become bastions of self-interest, unity is lost.

Conflict now flares when the flammable fluid of *violent language* is poured upon the smoldering coals to make ashes of human relationships and burn to the ground any hope for reconciliation. Sad to say, the case of the early church is not unfamiliar to us. Malicious murmurs spread like wildfire among the believers; Hellenists attack Hebrews and Hebrews counter against Hellenists. Violent language serves as the torch for their hate and the apostle James writes later, their "tongue is a fire" (James 3:6). Do you remember the boss who fired an employee with this wire, "You are incompetent, dishonest and stupid. *Harsh letter follows*"? How often the violence of language becomes the flaming agent that destroys the relationships between bosses and employees, husbands and wives, parents and children, presidents and professors, pastors and people.

Christian organizations are not exempt from conflict. Even in holy company, where resources are limited, roles are defined and relationships are verbal, the potential for conflict is ever-present. In fact, Christian organizations may be more susceptible to conflict because we know each other so intimately and care for each other so deeply. Issues that might remain objective in a secular setting take on personal overtones and subjective meaning. For instance, a vice-president came to our university from a public institution. After three years he asked for the privilege of returning to teaching with the explanation, "In the state university we would fight like cats and dogs and then forget it. Here in the

Christian university even a line item in the budget becomes
a personal issue." Too often, the classical components of
conflict play upon these differences, making the church budget a battleground, dividing a congregation and provoking
murmurs that paralyze the church.

SERVING BY PERSONAL EXAMPLE

When the early church got into this kind of trouble, the
apostles put out the call for servant-leaders to enter the
conflict, resolve the differences and get the church moving
again. Calling the whole company of believers together,
the apostles exercised sound management by suggesting
a division of labor with delegated authority to layleaders
called "deacons" to administer the food program.

One might expect that the apostles would call for persons
skilled in planning, organizing, staffing, coordinating, budgeting and reporting—functions that describe the role of
administrative leadership: None of these skills is mentioned
or inferred. According to our Scripture, the seven nominees
for servant-leadership were to be men of personal integrity,
practical wisdom and "filled with the Holy Spirit." John
Gardner in his book, *No Easy Victories*, advised that the
only qualifications you seek in leaders are ". . . taste and
judgment. Almost everything else can be bought by the
yard."[2] The apostles made a similar assumption about
Christian leaders. Putting character ahead of competence,
they sought only individuals of personal integrity, who were
filled with practical wisdom and the Holy Spirit—everything else was considered a dime a dozen.

Personal integrity is the first qualification for servant-
leadership. In the volatile climate of conflict and under
the scrutiny of murmuring factions, administrative matters
often turn into personal tests of credibility and character.
In these circumstances, servant-leaders are visible and vulnerable. When Billy Graham was in Seattle, Washington,

for his crusade in 1976, he withstood pointed cross-examination from a skeptical press. His wife, Ruth, told me that one reporter in particular proved to be the most bitter and biting man whom her husband had met in thirty years before the media. Dr. Graham felt as if he had failed with the man, but I knew the other side of the story. When the reporter returned from the press conference, he told his colleagues as he sat at his typewriter, "It won't be easy to attack Graham. The man is genuine." Visible leadership is the leading edge of the servant-leader's public witness and sometimes the court of last resort.

Practical wisdom is the second qualification for a Christian who leads by serving. Conflicts created by self-interested factions are never resolved until someone sees the "big picture" and envisions what psychologists call a "subordinate goal" to lift the sights of the battling factions. In the inner circles of the college presidency, we facetiously say, "Nothing ever happens in a faculty meeting until the president interprets the sense of the meeting." Even at the risk of faculty wrath, the point is well-taken. Practical wisdom is the combination of intuition, experience and homework that sees beyond the factions of self-interest to a larger purpose.

The popular book, *In Search of Excellence,* is a study of the best-run companies in America. In the preface, the authors confess that they began their study with the bias that leadership is not a critical factor in developing corporate quality. Their bias is instantly dispelled when they find a legendary leader with a concern for human values behind every excellent company. To illustrate the quality of that leadership, the authors cite a study that distinguishes between "world class" chess players and those who are a notch below, in the "championship" class. Both groups were shown scores of chess games in progress, each with a different situation on the board.

The researchers were astounded by the ability of the

world class players to see almost instantaneously the pattern of the complex chess game and make the strategic move. In contrast, championship chess players seemed to struggle with the situation and the next move. The difference? Believe it or not, they found that the world class chess players were estimated to have a perspective of 50,000 chess patterns which they immediately saw and to which they intuitively responded, whereas the championship players were limited to 5,000.[3] The practical wisdom of the "big picture" and the strategic move not only wins chess games and builds excellent companies, but also resolves human conflict in Christian organizations.

Yet leaders who try to serve by relying only upon their own personal integrity and practical wisdom operate in a small and shaky circle. For this reason, when the early church begins its executive search, only those who were *filled with the Holy Spirit* were eligible for election. Personal integrity, then, is no longer a matter of rigid self-discipline or clever public cover-ups. Do you remember Paul's dossier in the Philippian letter? He lists his impeccable credentials that qualify him as a leader of leaders among the Jews only to disclaim them all in favor of this testimony: ". . . not having my own righteousness, which is from the law, but that which is through faith of Christ, the righteousness which is from God by faith" (Phil. 3:9).

Under the power of the Holy Spirit, practical wisdom also takes on transformed meaning. Not only does faith fill in the mysteries of the patterns that are beyond human comprehension, but as James writes: ". . . The wisdom that is from above is first pure, then peaceable, gentle, willing to yield, entreated, full of mercy and good fruits, without partiality and without hypocrisy" (3:17).

The qualifications for servant-leadership are now complete. Through the infilling of the Spirit, we are called to lead and serve with a personal integrity and a practical wisdom that is not our own. As E. Stanley Jones says in his final book, *The Divine Yes*, Christ is not a signpost that points "Go this way"; He is the shepherd who says, "Follow Me."⁴ To lead is to serve by personal example.

SERVING WITH REDEMPTIVE RESULTS

Silence follows the deacons after their election. The Scriptures gives us no hint about their "affirmative action" plan for equalizing the distribution of food. We are not told how they brought the Greeks and Jews back together for the first Wesleyan-type love feast; and we have no idea how they changed the grating sound of the grumble into the hum of a note of joy. All we know is that reconciliation takes place and, once again, the church turns its attention toward world redemption.

For those of us who are enamored with internal processes and administrative procedures, the biblical silence is maddening. We have a lesson to learn. Managerial methods are important only as they lead to redemptive results. And internal reconciliation is essential, but only as a base for advancing the gospel and serving human need. We can take our cue from the New York taxicab driver who said, "It's not the driving I like, it's the people I run into."

If you want to renew your vision for the potential of the evangelistic church, read again the report on redemptive results in Acts 6:7. Here is what happens when the body of Christ is reconciled and its energies are focused upon its redemptive mission. One, ". . . *the word of God spread.*" The image ripples on a pond, with the word of God spreading into the world by ever-widening circles, or as Phillips translates, "gaining more and more ground." Two, ". . . *the number of disciples multiplied greatly in Jerusalem . . . .*" After Pentecost, it is reported that thousands were "added" to the church daily. Then, just before the conflict over the distribution of food, the mathematics of effective evangelism takes over as the church makes the exponential leap to "multiplying" numbers of people who believe on Jesus Christ. Significantly, after the in-

ternal conflict is resolved and the church returns to evangelistic outreach, the number of disciples begins multiplying once again. Three, ". . . *A great many priests
were obedient to the faith.* " The church, for the first time,
penetrates into a strategic center of power, even into the
hardcore priesthood of the established institutional
church.

Neither the potential nor the expectations for the church
have changed. Whether pastor or parishioner, our servant-
leader task is the same—*reconciliation* within and *redemption* without—as evidenced by the ever-widening numbers
and the ever-penetrating witness.

Our case study concludes with the rewards for the servant-leader. Stephen, a Greek and a layman, is described
at the time of his nomination for deacon as a person full
of faith and of the Holy Spirit. Now, in Acts 6:8, we are
informed that he is empowered to do great wonders and
miracles among the people. One of the rewards of leadership is the *discovery of new gifts for serving God.* In his
commentary on Acts, F. F. Bruce tells us that the title
"deacon," as used in our case study, is far more restrictive
than the way we use the title for ministerial office today.[5]
In the division of labor proposed by the apostles, Stephen's
role is better defined as a "giver of alms" or a "distributor
of food." Yet, from that servant-base, the cultivated gift
of his Grecian mind is discovered and he becomes the most
eloquent defender of the Christian faith. In fact, some scholars suggest that his speech before the Sanhedrin cut the
Gordian knot that tied the early church to the Jewish faith
and set the gospel free for world evangelization. What a
promising picture for leadership development in the church
today! Our greatest untapped resource may be in the hidden
gifts of the lay people whom we have limited to waiting
on tables.

Another reward for the servant who takes the risk of
leadership is the *opportunity to exalt Christ.* Accused of
blasphemy on a trumped-up charge before the Sanhedrin,
Stephen's face shines like an angel (Acts 6:15). Then,

against the fury of the mob that will stone him, Stephen turns his face upward and cries, "Look! I see the heavens opened and the Son of man standing on the right hand of God . . ." (Acts 7:56) and, at the moment of death, he calls upon God saying, "Lord Jesus, receive my spirit" (Acts 7:59).

In his inimitable way, C. S. Lewis catches the meaning of the shining face, the beatific vision and the commending spirit when he envisions a person so living in the reflective image of Christ that looking in a mirror he sees a face that is not his own. In the image of the exalted Christ, the servant-leader finds his glory.

Not by surprise, then, the servant of Christ who takes the risk of leadership is rewarded by the *continuity of Christian witness*. Sometimes only faith can see that reward, as in the case of Stephen whose clothes were laid at the feet of a young man named Saul. Wherever servant-leaders are in action, God's Word will not be lost and God's work will not be stopped. In the mantle passing from Stephen to Saul, servant-leaders win assurance that the gospel will be perpetuated through others whom God calls.

E. Stanley Jones, after whom Asbury Theological Seminary has named its School of World Mission and Evangelism, is renowned as a Spirit-filled world statesman for the gospel of Jesus Christ. At the age of eighty-nine, Dr. Jones suffered a massive stroke that left him paralyzed and speechless. In one of the last entries in his journal, he anticipates going to heaven and asking the Lord for just twenty-four hours in which to visit his friends who are there. Then he writes, ". . . I shall go up to Him and say, 'Haven't you a world somewhere which has fallen people who need an evangelist like me? Please send me there.' For I know no heaven beyond preaching the gospel to people."[6] In one choice sentence, E. Stanley Jones resolves the servant-leader paradox in the Spirit of the exalted Christ. To lead is to serve by personal example, and with the promise of redemption for needy people. For pastors who are servant-leaders, there is no other heaven.

VIII

Rebuilding Our Leadership

During the French Revolution, a general looked over his balcony at a river of people rushing through the streets toward the Bastille. Spinning on his heel, he shouted to his aide, "Quick! My tunic and my sword. I am their leader and I must follow them."

A pastor shares the general's dilemma. *"When do I lead and when do I follow?"* If the church were organized as a disciplined army marching in lockstep toward a single objective, there would be no conflict. Decisions about mission, goals, strategies and tactics would be made in the pastor-general's staff room. Every recruit for the church would learn to follow the two rules of military decision-making: *One,* the general is always right; *two,* if in doubt, obey the first rule.

Despite the vigor with which we sing "Onward, Christian Soldiers," a congregation is not an army. It is better described in the company of university faculties and hospital staffs. They are "organized anarchies." Some semblance of corporate structure is necessary to help them do their job, but professors and physicians remain stubbornly independent—sometimes bordering on anarchy. Because they are experts in their fields and colleagues with their leaders, professors and physicians refuse to be put into the square boxes or obey the black lines of authority on organizational charts. Whatever the issue, they are people who think otherwise.

Parishioners also think otherwise, but not for the same reasons as professors and physicians. They do not claim to be scholarly experts in theology or professional colleagues in the ministry with their pastor. Rather, they are independent because they are volunteers for the church who can leave at any time—and often do. More than that, parishioners are peers in Christ with their pastor. Before God, all persons are equal and in the Body of Christ, all persons are brothers and sisters. In management terms, the organization of the church is either "flat" or "round." Attempts to superimpose an organizational and hierarchical "pyramid" upon the church is to invite rebellion. For this reason, churches join with universities and hospitals as the most difficult of all organizations to lead. No wonder that a pastor looks out over the movement of his people, calls for the symbols of his ministerial authority and repeats the confused mumble of the French general, "I am their leader and I must follow them."

LEADER-FOLLOWER DILEMMAS

A pastor who is troubled by the contradictions of his leader-follower role needs to know that the conflict is inherent in the nature of the church. Behind the fact that a church is organizationally neither corporate fish nor chaotic fowl are the deeper dilemmas of *purpose, power* and *performance.*

At first thought, the *purpose* of a church seems precise

and clear. Obedient to The Great Commission, a church
is organized to preach the gospel and disciple believers.
But wait—compare the answer that you would get if you
asked a church member and a General Motors employee
the same question, "What is the primary purpose of your
organization?" Without hesitation, the General Motors employee would answer, "Produce cars at a profit." Immediately, an organizational pyramid designed "to produce cars
at a profit" comes to mind. Authority flows downward to
the assembly line through a division of labor; and responsibility moves upward to the Chairman of the Board through
the supervisory ranks. Everyone knows where the buck
stops. The Chairman of the Board either produces cars at
a profit or is replaced with only the mercy of a lifetime
pension.

No such simple answer can be expected from a church
member who is asked, "What is the primary purpose of
your organization?" If every Christian answered "Save
souls," the church might be organized like General Motors.
In that case, the pastor would have no leader-follower conflict. But alas, The Great Commission permits infinite variation on its interpretation. In contrast with the hard-nosed,
impersonal and singular purpose of General Motors, The
Great Commission for the church is an ideal involving people who cannot be stamped out on a spiritual assembly
line. The pastor is both victor and victim. He can lead with
the inspiration of The Great Commission and with the resources of the Holy Spirit, but neither fits an organizational
chart. Consequently, the purpose of the church is not a
closed issue and the practice of the church is not photo-
copied in heaven. To translate The Great Commission into
a working principle, the pastor must live with the contradiction of being a leader-follower.

Power is another dilemma for the pastor. By definition,
power is the ability to influence people and decisions in
an organization. Two facts about power affect the pastor's
leadership role. One is that *power may be formal or*

informal. Formal power is *positional influence*, usually represented by such symbols of authority as the general's tunic or the minister's gown. Informal power is *personal influence*, usually residing in an individual who may hold no position but has the power of persuasion. Every pastor has had the experience of working with a person who is the informal leader of the congregation. Without his or her approval, even the best of the pastor's recommendations will be contested, revised or defeated.

Power is also inelastic. The supply does not increase upon demand. Power is like a pie of a certain size. No matter how many pieces you may cut, there is only so much to go around. So, with each piece that is cut, someone's share is reduced.

In a highly structured organization, formal power rules. A military general or a corporate president will retain the dominance of formal power in order to counter any insurgence of informal leadership. Churches are different. A pastor shares his power, not only with his staff, but with lay leadership. In most churches, commissions and boards of laypersons will function like legislative bodies in a check-and-balance system upon executive leadership. The result is that the church is not an efficient organization. Just last week, a frustrated contractor told me that he had to pull his work crew away from a church remodeling job for three weeks because the building committee could not decide on the kind of windows they wanted in the foyer. Participatory democracy is priceless but costly.

A pastor's leadership role is impacted by the dilemma of shared power in a church organization. As the laity becomes more directly involved in the governance of the church, the pastor must take more responsibility for decisions that are not his own. Authority may be delegated to laypersons, but the pastor cannot delegate his responsibility. To add to the dilemma of shared formal power, the pastor must learn to lead by persuasion as well as by position. More and more, he will have to climb down from his

ministerial pedestal and contend for his position toe-to-toe
with an equally persuasive lay leader. In each case, the
traditional idea of pastoral dominance gives way to a leader-
follower role.

Performance is the third dilemma for pastors in the organization of the church. A popular cliché is, "It's what's
on the bottom line that counts." The term "bottom line"
comes from the profit-and-loss statement of a corporation
where presumably nothing but performance counts.

Churches are organized for process, not performance.
Like universities and hospitals, their concern is quality,
not quantity. Hospitals, for instance, are dedicated to
health, but no one expects them to publish a "bottom line"
report on wins and losses with life and death. Universities
are now resisting attempts to measure students on a quanti-
tative performance scale. Basic competencies in reading,
writing and speaking may be one thing, but who can measure the critical thought, the creative impulse or the moral
insight?

Performance in a church is equally hard to measure.
John Stott has called into question the "numbers game"
of conversions that has been promoted by some evangelistic
methods and church growth movements. Citing The Great
Commission, Stott contends that we are to go and preach
the gospel to all nations, but leave the results to God. In
other words, the "bottom line" belongs to God because spiritual results cannot be measured by human instruments.
If they could be, man would take the glory.

A leader is expected to be performance-minded and re-
sults-oriented. A pastor is no exception. This summer I
heard two laymen talking about their pastor. One compli-
mented his preaching and his pastoral care. The other answered, "Yes, but how many conversions have we had this
year?"

The dilemma takes an edge off the leadership identity
of the pastor. Like the general moving with the flow of
the crowd, a pastor who is in the process of ministering

to his people without being self-conscious about his performance may appear to follow as well as to lead.

THE LEADER-FOLLOWER FALLACY

How do we resolve the leader-follower dilemma for the pastor? Our tendency is to react like a drunk man trying to ride a horse. He gets up on one side only to fall off the other. So it is with simplistic theories of leadership. We assume that a pastor must either be a dominant leader or a passive follower.

Early in my administrative career, I became acquainted with the studies of leadership styles in education. Presidents of colleges and principals of schools were divided into two types of leaders—authoritarian and democratic. Authoritarian leaders were characterized as dictatorial, impersonal, noncommunicative and untouchable. Democratic leaders were just the opposite. They shared their power, cared about people, opened two-way communications and welcomed critical feedback. Every president and principal felt guilty. Presumably, a full-scale democratic administration was the only option for enlightened leaders and the only hope for an educational Utopia. But something was wrong. Later studies showed that some authoritarian leaders were as effective as their democratic counterparts and some democratic leaders failed as miserably as the authoritarians. Slowly, the lesson was being learned. Leadership style can never be cast in the concrete of "either-or" categories, especially for presidents of universities, administrators of hospitals and pastors of churches.

Still, the "either-or" tendency persists. Today, we are being told that the leadership of the future will be *transactional* rather than *transforming*. In his formidable volume, *Leadership*, James MacGregor Burns identifies transactional leaders as those who practice the art of participatory democracy and trade value for value in order to achieve their goals.[1] Like David Reisman's "other-directed man" in *The Lonely Crowd*,[2] transactional leaders have an ever-moving radar screen in their heads to pick up cues about group goals, needs and feelings before making recommendations or decisions.

In contrast, the transforming leader is an "inner-directed man" operating according to a built-in gyroscope from which he gets his goals and directions. Rather than leading by following political consensus and compromise, as in the case of the transactional leader, he relies upon some combination of authoritative position, charismatic personality, superior knowledge and far-sighted vision to rally support for his program.

LEADER-FOLLOWER PRINCIPLES

If a pastor cannot be stereotyped by an "either-or" style of leadership, what alternative do we have? One answer is that the pastor must be both leader and follower according to some proven principles.

First, follow in your strength, lead in your weakness. Contrary to some expectations, no pastor is perfect. Each of us brings strengths and weaknesses to our leadership task. Our natural tendency is to hold our strengths and delegate our weaknesses. Not so, according to management consultants. Ken Hansen, retired chairman of Servicemaster, says, "If you are to grow as an effective leader, you will delegate your strengths and develop your weaknesses." A pastor I know is strong in church administration, but weak in pastoral calling. Contrary to the rule for effective leadership, he assumed the executive role for the church and hired a minister of visitation. His administration was strong and no one was missed who needed a pastoral call. But then his sermons began to sound pedantic because he had lost touch with the needs of his people. If he had delegated his strength in administration to a church executive and accepted the challenge of his weakness, he would have been a more effective pastor.

Second, follow among leaders, lead among followers.
Churches, too, have personalities with strengths and weaknesses. Stationing committees of episcopal denominations
or selection committees of congregational churches do not
pay enough attention to the personality of the church in
appointing pastors. For instance, I became acquainted with
a church where the pastor had been forced to resign after
a period of mental exhaustion. At the root of the problem
was an incompatibility of personalities. Congregation leadership and informal power were in the hands of prominent,
professional lay leaders who expected to be intimately involved in church policy and decision-making. The pastor
was also a transforming leader with strong ideas backed
up by a powerful pulpit and a charismatic personality.
When he tried to proclaim the mission of the church in
his preaching, ego faced off against ego. Neither side would
give. Tension mounted until the pastor broke under the
strain and resigned. The congregation wanted a balloon-
holder, but got a shining star.

Horror stories about opposite situations could be told.
A mismatch between a pastor who is a transactional leader
and a congregation that expects transformational leadership will produce dissatisfaction for both parties and paraly-
sis for the church. Such disasters could be avoided if pastors
and congregations considered the leader-follower compatibility of the partners before the marriage took place.

Third, follow in calm, lead in crisis. Churches go through
the ebb and flow of calm and crisis. Leadership style must
change with the tide. In times of calm, congregations need
transactional pastoral leadership. Like a pause that re-
freshes, this is the time when the pastor and his people
can catch their breath and build strength into their personal relationships. At that time, a wise pastor will lead
by following.

Last week, a friend told me about a lesson in leadership
that he learned in the army. He was a member of a rifle
team practicing behind the lines. Flat on his stomach, he

fired round after round, stopping only long enough to reach
back over his shoulder for a re-load from an aide. Not until
he finished did he look back to see that his aide was a
full-bird colonel in dungarees face down in the dirt with
his troops. Later on, when the same colonel ordered his
men into battle, my friend said that every man was ready
to die for him.

In crisis, a transforming leader is needed. There is no
time for protracted discussions to find out which way the
congregation is going. Right or wrong, the pastor has to
make a decision. More often than not, the people will honor
him, particularly if he has become one of them during times
of calm.

Crisis leadership requires a skilled and experienced
leader. A management consultant compared leadership in
calm and leadership in crisis with flying an airplane. If,
during a smooth flight on automatic pilot, the captain receives word that a thunderstorm is three hundred miles
ahead, he has the time to go through all of the complicated
procedures for adjusting his course and averting the storm.
But if an engine fails upon takeoff, there is no time for
long-range planning. Instantly and intuitively, the captain
must act to avoid a crash.

A crisis in a church requires a similar kind of response.
People expect their pastor to have the skills and the intuition of experience to respond decisively for them in crisis.
They want an authoritative leader who has been a compassionate follower.

Fourth, follow in planning, lead in administration. Administration involves planning, organizing, staffing, directing, coordinating, reporting and budgeting. The "either-or"
fallacy assumes that the same leadership style applies to
each function. Disaster is the result. If parishioners are
like the members of other organizations, they expect to
participate personally and directly in the planning or goal-
setting function of the church. But then they expect an
administrator to carry out the plans through the functions

of organizing, staffing, directing, coordinating, reporting and budgeting! Frustration rises in any organization when the administrator seeks consensus for an executive decision that is already consistent with the plans and the goals of the group. Nothing ever gets done. Having followed in planning, a pastor must either lead or delegate with full authority the leadership for administration.

Fifth, follow in procedure, lead in principle. Whether we like it or not, pastoral leadership is political. We live in a day when leaders cannot bulldoze people or ramrod their programs. With other leaders, the pastor must learn to practice the art of the possible, including negotiation and compromise. Hackles will rise at the sound of the word "compromise" because pastors have the authority of "Thus saith the Lord." No one disagrees, but pastors cannot preach on every issue on the church agenda or turn on their pulpit voice in every board meeting. It is a misuse of the authority to preach the gospel when that authority is used to win when the pastor ought to compromise. Senator Mark Hatfield gave some guidelines for Christian leadership when he responded to the question about compromise in the political setting. His answer was that he frequently compromised on timing, wording and procedure, but never on principle.

Pastoral leaders can follow the same guideline. In the give-and-take over timing, wording and procedures for the work of the church, a pastor can afford to follow with compromise. His task, whether in the pulpit or in a board meeting, is to lead his people truthfully, tenderly and consistently with biblical principles. In the heat of campus revolt at Harvard in 1970, students demanded release from final examinations. The professors buckled under the pressure and gave "pass" or "fail" grades. After graduation, however, the students returned to complain about the lack of letter grades to help them compete for jobs. Befuddled, one professor asked a former student, "Why complain? We gave you what you wanted." "Yes, you did," the graduate

answered, "but just because we panicked, we didn't expect
that you would too."

A pastor can afford to compromise with timing, wording
and procedure in the political process of church business.
But when biblical principles are at stake, his people will
expect him not to panic.

Sixth, follow with people, lead with things. A pastor is
a steward of the resources of people, money, time, space
and knowledge. There is a difference among these resources.
A leader must use money, time, space and knowledge, but
develop people. The cardinal sin of leadership is to pervert
stewardship by *using people* and *developing things.*

Every congregation is rich in hidden, and often wasted,
human resources. An effective pastor will see the colorful
beauty in the individual gifts of his people, honor their
strengths and encourage their development as unique con-
tributors to the Body of Christ and to the mission of the
church. To do this, however, a pastor must first be efficient
in the use of the resources of money, space, time and knowledge. The gift of administration is a facilitating gift. Efficiency in the use of things frees a leader to be effective
in the mission of Christian nurture and evangelism. Our
model is the early church when the apostles elected deacons
to distribute food and wait on tables so that they could
give their undivided attention to prayer and preaching.

PRINCIPLES OF BODY LEADERSHIP

The deeper one probes into the leader-follower dilemma
of the pastor, the greater the understanding of "the body"
as the biblical model for the church. Usually, we inter-
pret the "body language" of Ephesians, 1 and 2 Corinthians and Colossians in relational and functional terms.
We cannot miss the meaning of the model for pastoral
leadership.

Compare the body with the "either-or" models that Peter
Drucker has used to illustrate extremes in organization.[3]

One is the amoeba—an organism like the body, but without an internal structure to make it efficient or purposeful. Every cell is in direct contact with the external environment and responsive to every change of stimuli in its surroundings. An amoeba is participatory democracy at its best, and its worst.

At the other extreme is the computer—not a living organism, but a machine that is totally dependent upon the facts which are fed into its electronic brain. A computer is a genius in efficiency, but an imbecile in effectiveness. In contrast with the amoeba, it is exclusively internal in its structure. A computer has no capability for responding to changes in the external environment unless the response is already programmed into its memory system. Organizationally, a computer is the ideal model for the dictatorship in Orwell's *1984*.

The church is neither an amoeba nor a computer. It is a Body—controlled by the head and tuned to a delicate balance between internal efficiency and external effectiveness. What part of the Body is the pastor? Is he not like the cerebellum, the center for communicating messages, coordinating functions and conducting responses between the head and the Body? If so, certain principles of Body Leadership follow. One is that *Christ is the Head* who controls the mind, will and spirit of the Body. Authority for the pastor is God's special call and gift to communicate the truth from the Head to the Body. As Paul wrote, "Such is the gospel of which I was made a minister, by God's gift, bestowed unmerited upon me in the working of his power" (Eph. 3:7, NEB). All communication, however, is two-way. The pastor is not only the *authoritative communicator of the truth* from the Head to the Body, but he is also the *accurate communicator of the needs* from the Body to the Head. Intercessory prayer for his people is the other side of the pastor's role as communicator. Thus, the pastor is an authoritative leader in communication, not an authoritarian leader of a system. The difference is that an authoritarian leader seeks to usurp the control of the Head rather than be a communicator for its messages.

In relationship to the members of the Body of Christ, the *pastor is the coordinator of their functions.* By God's design, human organisms seek wholeness and balance as a natural response. Like a body, the church needs the skeleton, the sinew, the respiratory and arterial systems of organization to achieve internal balance for growth. Paul had this in mind when he wrote to the Colossians, ". . . yet it is from the Head that the whole body with all its joints and ligaments, receives its supplies, and thus knit together grows according to God's design" (Col. 2:19, NEB). Functioning as a coordinator for the Head, the pastor has the responsibility to nourish the Body for its growth and balance the Body for its unity.

Now for the "bottom line." According to Ephesians 4:12, the gift of the pastor is given for the ". . . equipping of the saints for the work of the ministry, for the edifiying of the body of Christ." As communicator, he equips the Body; as coordinator, he edifies the Body. What about the "work of the ministry"? *Like the cerebellum, the pastor is the conductor for the response of the Body to the external world.* Of all social institutions, only the church has the primary purpose of serving people who are not its members. Once again, we are brought up short against The Great Commission. When all is said and done, the pastor's responsibility for "equipping . . . the saints" and "edifying the body" is for one, high-intensity purpose—to evangelize the world. Every pastor's performance will be judged on that "bottom line."

Body leadership saves the pastor from being either a "balloon-holder" or a "shining star." Even the idea of leader-follower is too bland to describe the strength and the beauty of the relationship between a pastor and his people in the Body of Christ. We need to rewrite the leadership role of the pastor as:

—Authoritative communicator of truth
for equipping the Body
—Efficient coordinator of functions
for edifying the Body
—Effective conductor of members
for evangelizing the world.

The biblical role of the pastor is the resolution of the leader-follower dilemma.

IX

Regulating Our Tasks

When lay leaders of churches are asked to cite the major weakness in the education of pastors, they most often answer, "church administration" or "management." Their perspective may be partially biased by the professional world from which they come. Nevertheless, if the pastor is to have the respect of the laity as a confident leader of an efficient church and an effective ministry, administrative skills are indispensable to the clerical role.

To most people, administration is a necessary evil. Carried over into the context of the church and the pastoral role, the attitude culminates in the skeptical question, "Is administration ministry?" Ideally, the answer is "Yes." In practice, though, the ministry of administration is occasionally denied, often divided and usually devalued.

Few people will intentionally deny administration as a ministry in the church. More often than not, denial comes from a limited definition of "ministry." After graduation from seminary, I took an administrative position as dean of men in a Christian liberal arts college. Arriving home from seminary, I was met on the steps by a saintly but semi-hysterical woman of the church, who wrapped her arms around me and wept, "Oh, oh, oh. I prayed so hard that God would lead you into the ministry." By limiting "ministry" to the pastorate, she denied me God's call to an administrative parish with 250 college men as members.

While most people do not go so far as to deny the ministry of administration, they would espouse a de facto split in Christian organizations that divides the ministry into sacred and secular parts. A recent seminary graduate tells of being greeted at his new pastorate with a job description stating that he was "to differentiate spiritual responsibilities from administrative responsibilities." In an eloquent rebuttal of that pre-Reformational attitude, the candidate says his response was to identify the Incarnation as God's entry into a mundane world—a world that includes administrative duties. His confrontation reminds us that the division between the "sacred" ministry of preaching and the "secular" ministry of administration is an attitude that still persists.

Even those who do not deny or divide administration as a ministry are prone to devalue its role in the kingdom of God. The attitude of devaluation is expressed by people who take for granted the results of effective administration or act as if the function is dispensable. Admittedly, good administration is neither dramatic nor visible. In fact, the most effective administrator is the one who gets the right things done through other people, even when it means seeing a personal idea come full circle with credit going to someone else. Seldom is an administrator thanked for doing a good job. Norman Cousins once asked Jawaharlal Nehru what he had learned after a lifetime of political leadership. Nehru answered, "People in politics must make known their gratitude to others for any generosity, however small, but they make a great mistake if they expect others to make known any gratitude for generosity to them, however large."[1]

On the other hand, an administrator is held accountable and criticized the moment that the support system breaks down. Abraham Lincoln, the most maligned president in American history, accepted criticism as part of his role. During the Civil War, he commanded General Meade to attack Lee's army with the following instructions: "The order I enclose is not a matter of public record. If you succeed, you need not publish it. If you fail, publish it. Then, if you succeed, you will get the credit; if not, I'll take the responsibility."

Lincoln did not suffer from paranoia or self-pity. As commander-in-chief, he accepted the reality of his executive role.

Administrators who see themselves as ministers are not exempt from the same reality. Their role is valued only as the primary mission of the church is achieved. Even then, no praise is to be expected and, if the mission is not accomplished, criticism will be the order of the day.

Is administration a ministry? Our original query has expanded into three key questions. Is administration an ordained or adjunct ministry of the church? Is it a sacred or secular function? Is it a primary or secondary task? Paul, the apostle, establishes the principles by which we can answer these questions. They come in his response to the controversy over spiritual gifts that threatened to destroy the infant church at Corinth. Paul's short treatise in 1 Corinthians 12 is an inspired statement on the nature and structure of the church in relation to the roles and functions of its members. If administration is a legitimate, spiritual and essential ministry of the church, it will be confirmed by these principles.

ORGANIZED TO MINISTER

Schism over the gift of tongues threatened to tear apart the Corinthian church. Some members abused this gift by making it the superior, if not the singular, sign of spirituality. Rather than directly attacking this twist of truth, Paul chooses to put the gift of tongues into the perspective of an "organizing and operating manual" for the church as a whole. The following spiritual principles are as sound for management theory as they are true for Christian theology.

I. *God, the Holy Spirit, is the purpose for the church, the center for its organization and the source of all spiritual gifts* (1 Cor. 12:3–6).

Every formal institution requires a reason for being, a focus for organization and a center for resources. Otherwise, like the double-minded man, it is unstable in all its ways, neither efficient nor effective. Therefore, before dealing with the diversities of the functioning church, Paul first proclaims the unity of believers. Not by accident, the preamble that guides the principles of organization and operation for the church is one of the landmarks of New Testament affirmation: ". . . no one can say that Jesus is Lord except by the Holy Spirit" (1 Cor. 12:3). Center of centers, the church in all its dimensions and diversities is sustained by the unifying confession, "Jesus is Lord."

II. *Members of the church, by the same Holy Spirit, have different gifts, ministries and operating styles* (1 Cor. 12:4–6).

The common confession, "Jesus is Lord," is like a stake driven deeply into the bedrock of belief. From this immovable center, then, the tether of diversity plays out to a circumference that encompasses infinite individual variation. Each person becomes a mathematical exponent of three— a different gift, a different ministry, a different operating style. And no two persons are alike. The result is a unified church that has infinite richness and unlimited potential among its members.

III. *God, the Holy Spirit, endows each person with one of His special gifts: wisdom, knowledge, faith, healing, miracles, prophecy, discernment, tongues or interpretation of tongues* (1 Cor. 12:7–11).

If God's revelation of special gifts is taken seriously, it will change the way in which we look at people. Rather than looking for the faults to criticize, we are to look for the gift of the Holy Spirit that we can encourage and cultivate. Rather than leaving the witness of the Holy Spirit as a generalized experience of cleansing and filling, we are to see its expression in a specific gift that contributes uniquely to the ministry of the church.

These special gifts are not roles to be played nor functions to be performed; they are spiritual traits natural to the person, integral to the life of the church and functional to its mission. C. S. Lewis, in his sermon, "The Weight of Glory," preaches to this conclusion when he says, "I have never met a common man." Isn't this the way in which Paul looks at Timothy when he encourages him to ". . . fan into flame the gift of God, which is in you through the laying on of my hands" (2 Tim. 1:6, NIV)?

IV. *God, the Holy Spirit, gives different gifts, ministries and operating styles to different people for the common good* (1 Cor. 12:7).

Diversity is not without accountability. Ultimately, every gift, ministry and style in the church must be tested against the standard of the "common good." It is a term that speaks of interpersonal relationships and institutional accomplishments. Paul spells out the "common good" in Ephesians when he says that the purpose of spiritual unity and functional diversity is ". . . to prepare God's people for works of service, so that the body of Christ may be built up until we all reach unity in the faith and in the knowledge of the Son of God and become mature, attaining to the whole measure of the fullness of Christ" (Eph. 4:12–13, NIV).

Each gift, each ministry, each operating style is to be judged by these results. Does it prepare God's people for works of service? Does it build up unity in the Body of Christ? Does it lead toward maturity according to the measure of Christ? Taken together, these standards total the "common good" of God's purpose in bestowing gifts, ordaining ministries and indulging personal styles.

V. *All of the diverse gifts, ministries and styles in the Body of Christ are integral to its harmony and essential to its effectiveness* (1 Cor. 12:12–27).

No analogy in Scripture withstands scrutiny for clarity and consistency better than the Body of Christ. Paul does not let the principles of organizational unity and operating diversity for the church become static and technical; instead, he is inspired to put them to work in the dynamic context of an organic model—the human body. In doing so, he makes harmony the prime focus for the healthy, functioning organism. Harmony is thrown out of balance if: (1) a part of the body is mistaken for the whole; (2) the weaker parts are assumed to be dispensable; and (3) the ugly parts are despised or given no honor. Each is a fallacy and contrary to the interactive harmony that God has built into the human body and desires for the spiritual body. No gift is, in and of itself, the whole Body of Christ; no ministry is independent of other ministries; no operating style is without value to the harmony of the whole. "Equal concern" in suffering or in honor is the homeostatic balance of the Body in the church of Jesus Christ.

VI. *God organizes the church by appointing to special office, apostles, prophets and teachers; and to special work, healers, helpers, administrators and speakers in tongues* (1 Cor. 12:27–28).

Advocates of a "flat" organization in which there are no vertical distinctions in roles and functions within the church, will be disappointed by this hierarchy of spiritual offices and functions. Paul makes God's strategy obvious: If the Corinthians had operated strictly from the church's organizational chart before the spiritual principles of unity in diversity were established, then the order of special offices and functions would have read like a "pecking order" for prestige. This would have been the *coup de grâce* for the tension-filled Corinthian church. Now, however, the truth can be told. The Body of Christ not only has a division of labor, but a scale of importance for its ministries. Positioning on that scale is determined by the proximity of the role to the proclamation of the Word of God. Accordingly, apostles who heard Jesus speak the Word are first, preachers of the Word are second and teachers of the Word are third. Here, the special offices of ministry end.

All other ministries are functions based upon the special gifts of healing, helping, administering and speaking in tongues. By organizational placement, these special gifts are given as support functions for the special offices of the apostle, prophet and teacher. Gently, but decisively, Paul informs the Corinthians that the gift of tongues, which they have exalted and made exclusive, is the least gift of all.

>   VII.   *Whatever general or special gift the Holy Spirit*
>   *gives a person, higher gifts can be sought and*
>   *received* (1 Cor. 12:28–31).

Paul could have left his readers floundering in the despair of having been knocked from the top to the bottom rung on the ladder of spiritual gifts. Instead, he offers them the incentive to ". . . eagerly desire the greater gifts" (1 Cor. 12:31, NIV). In all of His dealings with men, God holds out the promise of growth toward a higher goal. Interpreters of tongues can become speakers in tongues; speakers in tongues can become administrators; administrators can become helpers of people; helpers can become healers; and healers can become miracle workers.

What about a promotion from a special function to a special office in the church? Again, the deacon Stephen serves as our model. Elected as an administrator, he becomes a prophet in the court of the Sanhedrin and dies with an apostolic vision before his eyes. Miracle workers can become teachers, teachers can become prophets, and prophets can become apostles through a vision of the living Christ. Promotion, however, is not a human prerogative. Paul writes, "All these are the work of one and the same Spirit, and he gives them to each man, just as he determines" (1 Cor. 12:11, NIV).

> VIII. *Love is the highest gift of the Holy Spirit,*
> *available to all, and indispensable to the*
> *internal harmony and external effectiveness of*
> *the Body of Christ* (1 Cor. 12:31).

In the Body of the Christian church, Christ is the head, believers are the organic parts, ministries are the skeleton and love is the lifeblood. Without self-sacrificing love coursing through the arteries and veins to nourish every cell in the Body of Christ, discord displaces harmony and ridicule rules over effectiveness.

Paul knows that neither revelation nor reason will prevail with the Corinthians unless they are gifted with love. Thus, his organizing and operating manual for the church comes full circle. Only as the Holy Spirit prompts us to confess, "Jesus Christ is Lord," are we open to love, the highest and the greatest gift of God. Without the gift of love, the Body of Christ breaks down. In sum, then, the apostle Paul gives us an organizing and operating manual for the church to function as the sound and effective Body of Christ.

GIFTED TO GOVERN

We now have the framework within which to ask our original question, "Is administration an ordained, sacred and essential ministry of the church?" When we apply the organizing and operating principles of 1 Corinthians 12 to this question and utilize the election of the seven deacons in Acts 6 as a case study, our response is guided by a series of working premises.

Premise One: Administration is a specialized function in the ministry of the church, an endowed gift for guiding people by organization and management.

At the end of his treatise on the organization of the church, Paul identifies the ". . . gift of administration" as a specialized function to which God appoints people for the ministry of the church (1 Cor. 12:28). Other translations of the same Scripture include such terms as "governments" (KJV), "organizers" (Phillips) and "power to guide" (NEB). The derivative meaning of the root word for administration in the Greek is "to steer," a picturesque reference to the pilot or helmsman of a ship. Consistent with the role of the administrator, the pilot is at the point of control for directing the crew and guiding the ship. In management theory, an efficient administrator is the one who gets the most out of people; an effective administrator is the one who best achieves the organizational goals. Both efficiency and effectiveness are included in the biblical definition of administration.

Premise Two: Power is the primary resource and justice is the primary responsibility for the ministry of administration.

Keen insight is given in the New English Bible, which translates the gift of administration as ". . . the power to guide (others)." Power, in the form of delegated author-ity, is the common resource that all administrators share. By definition, power can be *inferred, ascribed or earned.* A child, born into a line of succession to be a king or queen, is the recipient of *inferred power* by birth. A president, who takes a solemn oath, has *ascribed power* by virtue of his office. A person without title or office, who leads people through crisis, will often be recognized as a leader with *earned power.*

Scripture makes no provision for inferred power, except in the case of Jesus Christ, who was born as the Son of God. Rather, all power given to men is ascribed by God. This is a truth that administrators who are ministers must never forget. Those who acknowledge that their power is ascribed find administration a humbling task and a joyous honor. Those, however, who assume that their power is an inherent right or an earned privilege, usurp God and open the door to tyranny. The reason for this is simple: justice is the primary responsibility of administration as a ministry; rulers of government are to be recognized as ministers of justice, ". . . God's servant[s] to do you [us] good . . ." (Rom. 13:4, NIV).

For all who have the power to guide others, Paul sets justice as the standard for responsible administration when he sums up his advice to Timothy: "I charge you, in the sight of God and Christ Jesus and the elect angels, to keep these instructions without partiality, and to do nothing out of favoritism" (1 Tim. 5:21, NIV). The ministry of administration is a weighty responsibility because the one who possesses the power to guide others is accountable to God for the just exercise of that power.

Premise Three: Wisdom is God's special gift for the ministry of administration.

Wisdom is the special gift of the Holy Spirit that an administrator needs to keep the mission clear, hold power in check and keep justice in view. Organizations, even the Body of Christ, are made up of individuals and groups that are forever pulled toward self-interest. The ministry of administration is a balancing act upon these interests.

Wisdom is the special gift of God that helps an administrative leader "see the vision, state the mission and set the tone" for the church.

Premise Four: Administration is a support ministry to help members achieve the primary purpose of the church.

The principle of essentiality has already been established for administration as a ministry in Paul's analogy in the Body of Christ. All organs are interacting and all functions are integrating with the "common good" for the whole and living church. It is the "common good" that Paul sets forth as the end against which all gifts, ministries and operating styles are to be judged (1 Cor. 12:7).

Paul's emphasis upon the "common good" contains a warning: the ministry of administration is never an end in itself. There is a natural tendency for administrators to build organizational empires. The temptation of power is to manipulate people, advance oneself and to be "number one." To protect against these occupational hazards, an administrator must never forget that he or she is called to be a servant in a support role. Consider how Paul distinguishes between special offices and special functions in the church and then lists the ministries in order of priority. By category, administration is not a special office equal to the ministry of apostles, prophets and teachers. By priority, administration is not a special function that supersedes miracle-working, healing and helping others. In truth, administration is a lesser gift, positioned just ahead of speaking in tongues. Yet, remembering the Body principle of harmony, we see that administration is not to be denied, divided or despised. It is an essential ministry of support dedicated to the goal of the "common good," and necessary as long as human beings make up the church.

Premise Five: Administration is a ministry that opens up the potential for seeking and receiving higher gifts.

Immediately ahead of the gift of administration on the scale of special functions in the church is the gift of helping others. As a long-time Christian college administrator, I know what it means to seek the higher gift. My graduate study prepared me intellectually for articulating and implementing a philosophy of Christian higher education. Developing policy and programs consistent with that philosophy represented the achievements of my early career. After a seven-year stint at one Christian college, I received an invitation to move to a larger sister institution. During the searching moment of decision-making, I looked back upon my administrative career and realized that the lasting values are found in the changed and growing lives of a few students whom I had influenced. While endowed with the gift of administration, I yearned for the gift of helping others.

Later on in the second presidency, I assumed I would advance in my administrative career in five-year steps. At the end of five years, however, a wise counselor told me that it takes five years in an administrative position to implement a program and seven or more years to influence people. Fourteen years later, I left for my third presidency in Christian higher education, firm in the philosophy that effective administration is the twofold ministry of developing policy and developing people.

Stephen, the administrative deacon of the early church, continues to be my encouragement for seeking higher gifts. After he resolves the conflict over food distribution and normalizes the steps to assure that the people receive fair portions, Stephen challenges the Sanhedrin with a sermon. It is an address that taps every gift of the Holy Spirit and advances him through the ministries of the church to apostolic stature. Stephen's action cries out that the path to higher gifts and larger ministries is open to all administrators. If Stephen gives us our living example of administrative service, then Paul gives us our future goal when he says that deacons ". . . who have served well gain an excellent standing and great assurance in their faith in Christ Jesus" (1 Tim. 3:13, NIV).

Is administration a ministry? The question is now rhetorical. Ordained by the power of God, sealed by the wisdom of the Holy Spirit and dedicated to the common good, the gift to govern is a valid, sacred and essential calling, well worthy of the title, "Minister."

X

Recognizing Our Limits

One of my most impish questions for pastors is "What are your limits?" The answer usually comes back in shock waves of disbelief, insult and hurt. After all, the pastor is called to go into all the world with the unlimited power of the Holy Spirit. Doesn't the admission of limitations cast doubt upon our ministerial mandate and deny the power of Christ's personal promise?

I learned the lesson of limitations the hard way. Unbounded pride accompanied my first proposal for a doctoral dissertation. Its scope covered the whole field of higher education, its complexity required the most sophisticated statistical measures and its goal was to revolutionize administrative theory. My advisor saw it differently. After scanning the proposal, he sent it back to me with a single word on the cover, *"Delimit."* Three days later I recovered from my disappointment and began to slay the darlings of my research design. The scope was narrowed, the sample population was reduced, the statistics were simplified and the goals restricted. I felt as if my contributions to the scholarly world had been emasculated by insensitive fiat. But once again, after reading the revised proposal, my advisor sent it back with the expanded message, "Delimit more." Hurt turned to anger as I went back to cut the heart out of my study. The second revision went in with the assurance that no one could achieve the doctorate with anything less. This time my advisor called me in to explain the meaning of the word "delimit" in scholarly research. The best studies, he explained, are ridiculously singular in purpose and simple in design. "Go back and revise it with that goal in mind," he explained. "You will not be sorry."

How right he was. Today I do not look back upon my doctoral dissertation with scholarly pride. It is still too complicated; I tried to do too much. Yet I learned one of the lasting lessons of my life—*the law of delimitation*, which tells us that if we want to do something significant, we will be singular in our purpose and simple in our plan. Later when I became a professor in the same university, my office became the diagnostic center to which other professors referred their doctoral students who were suffering from the symptoms of scholarly megalomania in the design of their dissertations.

Through the years I have carried the word "delimit" into my career in Christian higher education as a president and consultant. In my first presidency, the law of delimitation was reinforced by a consultant who asked me the question for our college, "What's the big idea?" He meant that a small Christian liberal arts college with limited resources would gain its integrity and its quality by the discipline of a singular and simple purpose.

Just recently I served as a consultant for a small Christian college seeking regional accreditation. My assignment was to assist the school in reducing an overextended and uneconomical curriculum. Expecting a quick fix, the faculty was surprised when I started with the question, "What's the big idea?" Prompted by the question, however, the faculty became invigorated by the opportunity to rethink and restate the mission of the college in simple and singular terms. Unusual agreement brought the faculty together on a restatement of their mission. And with equal enthusiasm they subjected the curriculum to the discipline of asking, "How does this program contribute to our big idea?" Difficult decisions were made, some immediate and some long-range. The reward came, however, when the college was granted regional accreditation because of its ability to delimit its curriculum with the discipline of its institutional mission.

The law of delimitation is now being applied as a distinguishing characteristic in the studies of effective leadership. In the admittedly "small, expensive and invaluable" bestseller entitled *The One-Minute Manager*, the singularity and simplicity of one-minute goal-setting is extolled. As tough as it seems, the advice is that if you have more than one goal, you have too many goals. Also, a goal statement should be no longer than 250 words or one page typed double-space in length and readable in one minute.[1] As simplistic as the advice may be, I could see the wisdom of the word "delimit" written over the pages.

Megatrends, another best seller, evokes the law of delimitation when the author, John Naisbitt, poses the question of how organizations can cope with the cataclysmic changes brought on by the coming Age of Information. Naisbitt says the answer is for leaders of the organization to ask the question, "What business are we in?"[2] Unless that delimiting question is continuously asked, organizations will tend to venture beyond their expertise, overextend their resources, forget the reason for their initial success and drown in the backwash of social change. Book after book is now being written about effective leaders and successful organizations who share one common characteristic: they are disciplined by a founding principle that is singular and simple.

The law of delimitation needs to be enacted for the pastoral ministry. Church growth, program development, planned expansion and auxiliary services are in vogue at the present time. The assumption is that growth is good. Few pastors or congregations, however, are stopping to ask, "What business are we in?" The proliferation of church-related day care centers is an example. As chairman of the planning division of the Greater Bluegrass United Way, I noted our survey of day care centers in the area showed seventy-nine centers, most of which were church-related. Duplication of services was common, coordination was unknown and other human service needs, such as those of latch-key kids, went unmet. Furthermore, in most cases, the day care programs were poorly integrated into the ministry of the church. One can only surmise that dollars, prestige or popularity dictated the decision to establish the service without researching the need. If the question had been asked, "What business are we really in?" the answer might have been a delimiting decision.

As hard as it may be upon our preconceptions about Jesus, He serves as an example of a minister who recognizes His limitations. In fact, the effectiveness of Jesus' ministry is directly related to the limits He accepts and within which He works—the limits of time, space, energy, knowledge and achievement.

THE LIMIT OF TIME

Jesus' public ministry encompasses just three-and-a-half years or forty-two months, equaling the warm-up time for most ministries today. Within this brief period, He finishes the task of establishing the principles for the kingdom of God on earth, prepares disciples to perpetuate the gospel and leaves the drama of the cross and the power of the resurrection as His eternal contribution to God's redemptive plan. With the knowledge that His time is limited, Jesus honors its urgency but never succumbs to its tyranny.

At the beginning of His ministry, Jesus announces the urgency of time with the words, "The time is now, the kingdom is at hand, repent and believe the gospel." Yet, during His ministry when the masses clamor to make Him king, He responds with patience, "My time is not yet come." But then, when the issues are drawn and the end is inevitable, Jesus urges Judas, "What you do, do quickly." Many times in His last days He acknowledges, "My hour is come."

Jesus has a maturity of attitude toward time which few of us know until later middle age. In our youth, we assume that our time is unlimited and that our potential knows no bounds. Then we awaken to the realization that time has turned from friend to enemy. What we do, we must do quickly. A youth-oriented culture is particularly hard on aging egos. Bill Bradley, the all-pro basketball player who became a U.S. Senator, likens retirement of a professional athlete who is in his mid-thirties to a form of death itself. With active playing time averaging about four years in length, an athlete has limited time to achieve lofty goals and at the same time prepare for a radical change of careers. Time is a resource that must be effectively managed, not wasted.

In His ministry, Jesus puts into practice three principles of time management which experts recommend today. *First, Jesus plans His limited time.* Examples are plentiful. Planning takes Jesus from village to village for His preaching and healing ministry with the poor. Planning takes Him north and south across Galilee and to Judea and to the borders of Samaria. Planning keeps Him from entering Jerusalem for a confrontation with the Pharisees until His hour is come.

Second, Jesus eliminates nonessentials in His limited time. Critics who score Jesus for His lack of humor and playfulness do not understand the intensity of time under which He worked. His love for dinner parties, His leisurely times with Martha, Mary and Lazarus and His satirical repartee with the Pharisees tell us that He is not the "pale, gray Galilean" condemned by Nietzsche. As a storyteller par excellence, Jesus would have been a delightful conversationalist around the village cracker barrel or after the evening meal. The urgency of time, however, limits His small talk and eliminates the nonessentials from His life and ministry.

Third, Jesus delegates authority to conserve His limited time. Earlier we marvelled at His decision to send the disciples out two-by-two for preaching, teaching and healing even before they seemed to be ready for the assignment. Time as well as trust are at work in this decision. With the knowledge that His ministry might be interrupted momentarily, Jesus sets at work the principle of delegating the authority for His task at the beginning, not at the end, of His ministry.

Recognizing the limits of time is essential to the renewal of our ministry. No profession has so much discretionary time as the ministry. Yet, time management is a frustration for many ministers. Just to apply the principles of planning our time, eliminating the nonessentials of our task and delegating our authority will not only increase our efficiency but give us new satisfaction in the job as well.

THE LIMIT OF SPACE

Jesus has become such a universal figure that we forget the limits of the space in which He worked. Scholars estimate that He never traveled more than 200 miles from His hometown of Nazareth. In an age of instantaneous global communication and interstellar travel we have lost the value of spatial limits. Yet, space is an all-important resource that creates our personality and dictates our ministry. On 125th Street in Harlem, for example, the human population is so dense that crime and violence are part of survival. On a larger scale, sociologists suggest that America's social problems multiplied when the frontier closed and malcontents stayed home rather than moving on.

Jesus turns limited space into a valued resource in His ministry. When the synagogue becomes too small, He takes to the streets; when the streets become too small, He takes to the fields; and when the fields become too small, He takes to a boat. Yet, He stays within the confines of Israel. Saturation of limited space is a working principle for His ministry.

Few pastors see limited space as a resource to be cultivated. Pastors of downtown churches, for example, which have been squeezed by urban development, still try to create a program for surburban congregations. One pastor of a wealthy but aging and shrinking city church has never accepted the fact that he cannot establish a vigorous and expanding youth program. Each day, however, he looks out of his pastoral study upon a forest of high-rise apartments and high-priced condos which house thousands of adult singles and couples. Theoretically, he talks about ministry to these neighbors, but the conversation always lapses back into the frustration of limited space. If only he could see the potential for high return in his ministry with a relatively low investment of time and energy because of the value of limited space. Following Jesus' strategy, the pastor would trace and retrace his steps through that "gentrified" city area, searching out human need with the advantage of being able to saturate the space with the good news of the gospel.

THE LIMITS OF ENERGY

We have already established the principle of total well-being as a goal for the pastor. Emphasis was placed upon developing a rhythm of life involving work, worship, play and rest. We also noted that Jesus demonstrates this principle in the balance He created between His self-giving public ministry and His regenerating solitude. With His disciples, Jesus applies the same principle. After they return from their first preaching and healing mission without Him, Jesus urges them, "Come aside . . . and rest" (Mark 6:31).

The conservation of energy, particularly after periods of intensive ministry in which the total self is sacrificed and every strength is sapped, becomes a companion principle with a rhythm of life. Recognizing the limits of physical energy is necessary to coordinate maximum strength with the most essential tasks.

Age has a direct bearing upon energy levels. During my graduate school days, I prided myself on the ability to come intellectually alive after midnight. Today in middle age my mind turns to mush after the eleven o'clock news. My most creative thoughts and productive writings come in the early morning hours. If I try to handle administrative matters in the morning with the thought of writing in the afternoon or evening, I am invariably frustrated. Therefore, applying the principle of energy conservation, I have reprogrammed my working days to write in the early morning, administer during the midday and read at night.

The same principle of limited energy applies to group meetings. At a recent church conference, the general assembly met briefly to organize into committees. Two days and two nights of working sessions in committees followed. Then, when the general assembly reconvened, the order of the day was to deal with the resolutions that had been rejected. Laboriously, the committees began reporting their recommendations one by one. Anyone experienced in group dynamics and legislative process can predict the outcome. In the closing sessions of the conference, exhausted delegates will be asked to debate and decide major issues that will affect the direction of the denomination for years to come. At the midnight hour in the closing session, critical matters will be referred to an executive board for action and in so doing the general assembly will default on the democratic process. One look at the agenda prompted me to conclude, "The first action of the conference should be to establish a committee on priorities so that the most important issues can be debated while the delegates are fresh." The law of conservation for limited energy has many applications for ministry.

THE LIMITS OF KNOWLEDGE

Preachers who proclaim the Word of God are tempted to become oracles of truth on all subjects. Particularly as pastors gain visibility in the community, they are expected to address any controversial issue in the moral realm. It is unusual to hear a pastor say, "I don't know," or "The question is beyond my realm." Jesus, however, does not hesitate to give either answer. He confesses the limits of His knowledge of the end time when He says, "But of that day and hour no one knows, neither the angels in heaven, *nor the Son*, but only the Father" (Mark 13:32).

Applying that principle of limited knowledge to His teaching of the disciples, Jesus says, "I still have many things to say to you, but you cannot bear them now" (John 16:12). For this reason Jesus promises the Holy Spirit to guide the disciples ". . . into all truth" (John 16:13). Christ, the final revelation of God, does not see a contradiction to progressive knowledge about God. To recognize the limits of our knowledge is to open up realms of truth that otherwise we would never know. With limited knowledge we search, with limited knowledge we learn, with limited knowledge faith takes hold.

Within days after Charles Colson gained release from prison he appeared as a "born-again" celebrity guest of a group of evangelical church leaders in Washington, D.C. Colson stepped from the wings of the auditorium smoking a cigarette—a violation of the image of an evangelical Christian. I thought, *His conversion must be genuine*. In giving his testimony he mixed his new language of "Hallelujah" with his old language of "damn." I thought, *His conversion has to be genuine*. Then when members asked him theological and ecclesiastical questions, Colson answered, "I don't know." I exclaimed to myself, "There is no doubt; *he is genuine*."

Only the experience of the new birth could transform the hatchet man of the White House, who had all of the answers, into an honest and humble spirit confessing, "I don't know." While Colson's autographed biographical books *Born Again* and *Life Sentence* may be more popular, to me the most significant of his writings is the volume entitled *Loving God*. It is a sound and clear statement of his faith based upon his serious study of biblical theology which is motivated by his confession, "I don't know." To recognize the limits of knowledge is to fuel the desire to know the mind of Christ.

THE LIMITS OF ACHIEVEMENT

Critics of the American mind see a serious flaw in the success syndrome that has become an obsession with us. Fashioned out of the great American dream, we see ourselves in the image of Prometheus perpetually carrying fire to the mountain top. Consequently, any setback to our success—whether losing the race to the moon, coping with presidential assassination, facing defeat in Vietnam, driving a president out of office, waiting in gas lines, failing to free hostages or being beaten by foreign imports—is almost more than we can handle.

Pastors are not immune from the tyranny of success. Idealistic expectations about achievement make any flaw or failure a trauma of major proportions. To bring realism back into these expectations, we need to refer again to the ministry of Jesus. According to the success syndrome, He was a failure. He did not win the movers and shakers of His day or the institutions they represented. The masses that He won by miracles turned against Him in crisis. He was betrayed by His own disciple and died the most humiliating death known to mankind. Even though there were rumors of His resurrection, He left His disciples hiding in an upper room in fear of reprisal. Only the Son of God could declare His mission accomplished and only history could pass judgment upon His declaration to His Father, "I have finished the work you have given Me to do." In human terms and human times, Jesus lived with the limits of achievement.

Even in the secular world, a reaction is rising to the success syndrome. Few great leaders come to fame and power along a career line of unmitigated success. The autobiography of Lee Iacocca, for instance, has sold more than three million copies, making it one of the best-selling books of all time. As the folk hero who saved Chrysler Corporation from bankruptcy, Iacocca is the epitome of success. But in his autobiography, he sees as the turning point of his career the day he was summarily fired as the president of the Ford Motor Company.

Other studies of leadership reinforce the same point. Bennis and Nanus in their book *Leaders* find the ability to learn from failure an essential characteristic of effective leadership. As we noted earlier, leaders do not think of winning versus losing, but rather failure versus learning. As risk takers, they accept failure as an occupational hazard. They also believe that failure is actually failure only if you do not learn from the experience. Jesus teaches His disciples the same lesson. They could have been devastated by their failure to heal the epileptic boy. Instead, they dare to ask the question, "Lord, why could we not cast him out?" Jesus responds affirmatively and constructively, "This kind comes out only by prayer and fasting."

Every pastor must learn to live with the limits of achievement even when defined as failure. The question is whether failure destroys us or we learn from it. Furthermore, we must realize that success itself is a seductive siren which woos us to destroy us. Michael Maccoby, in his book entitled *The Gamesman*, surveyed corporate and institutional leaders who were identified with the symbols of success—salary, status and security. Still, he found in them an emptiness that could only be described as "spiritual."[3] Perhaps Maccoby's finding explains why a later study of future leaders revealed a disinterest in success as an end in itself. The leaders of tomorrow put a premium upon working relationships and personal commitments even at the expense of salary and status. They did, however, want security.

Pastors who strive for the standards of success in

ministry will fail because tangible reward becomes an end
in itself. Numbers and dollars, status and security have
insatiable appetites that can never be satisfied. John Stott
gives us the biblical standard for our ministry when he
says that the results are not our business. Our task is to
do the will of God and leave the results to the Holy Spirit.
Mother Teresa spoke the same truth when Senator Mark
Hatfield asked her, "How can you go out on the streets
of Calcutta, day after day, to minister to the sick and dying,
when you can never meet the need?" She answered, "The
Lord does not call us to be successful; He calls us to be
faithful." Failure isn't a word in Mother Teresa's vocabu-
lary. Faithfulness is. Therefore, from God she learns and
by the world she is honored.

Recognizing our limits is a sign of strength, not weakness.
In fact, there is a direct relationship between the clarity
of our mission and the recognition of our limits. Again,
we refer to Jesus as our example. When He stands up in
the synagogue to declare His redemptive mission, He draws
the limits of preaching as His method, the blind, broken,
bound and bruised as His mission field, the gospel as His
message and the joy of the jubilee year as His keynote.
In modern marketing terminology, Jesus "positions" Himself as unique among the people. To delimit His method
of preaching, He separates Himself from the social revolu-
tionaries who are trying to overthrow the Roman regime
by force. To delimit His mission field to the poor, He cuts
Himself away from religious ritualists who cater to the
wealthy and powerful. To delimit the gospel as His message,
Jesus distinguishes Himself as the fulfillment of the prophets' message. To sound the delimiting note of joy, Jesus
stands alone above the gloom and doom of the oppressive
religious, political and social climate of His day. To apply
the law of delimitation to our ministry is to "position" ourselves for effective action.

Recognizing our limits, therefore, needs to be viewed as
a resource, not a handicap. The analogy of the laser beam
illustrates the difference. Light that is disbursed for seeing

is valuable. To restrict it may be considered a handicap because darkness is increased as the beam of light is narrowed. But if the intensity of the light is focused into the microscopic beam of a laser, power is created to penetrate steel or heal a tumor. To delimit the light, then, is to utilize the power of its intensity for a specific task. Disbursed light has a function of dispelling darkness but only delimited light has the penetrating power to destroy or heal.

Pastors who feel as if their ministry is coming unraveled need to ask the question, "What are my limits?" Whether time, space, energy, knowledge or achievement, the limits can be drawn as a resource to concentrate our efforts and increase our effectiveness. We often think of Jesus being tempted by Satan to refute His redemptive mission. Satan is too subtle for that. More often than not, the test comes in the form of a temptation to dilute His ministry by going beyond the limits that He had accepted for Himself. One example stands out. As the foreboding clouds of crucifixion are lowering over Jesus' soul, His excited disciples tell Him that the Greeks want to see Him. For an untutored carpenter's son from the despised village of Nazareth, the news comes as a supreme form of flattery. Without doubt, Jesus is tempted to broaden His ministry to include the intellectual and cultural elite of the Gentile world. His struggle with the temptation to extend the limits of His ministry is felt in the wrenching words,

> Now My soul is troubled,
> and what shall I say?
> "Father, save Me from this hour'"?
> But for this purpose
> I came to this hour.
> Father, glorify Your name.
> (John 12:27–28)

For us, as well, whenever the temptation comes to broaden the limits that concentrate our ministry upon God's specific mission for us, we will find renewal in the firm declaration, "For this purpose I came to this hour. Father, glorify Your name."

XI

Reporting Our Results

As an eight-year-old boy sitting under the thundering ministry of a visiting evangelist, I first heard the phrase, "age of accountability." Extrapolating his doctrine from Jesus' first visit to the Temple, the evangelist told us that we became accountable for our sins at the age of twelve. A sigh of relief passed through me as the guilt for my childhood transgressions was lifted and I anticipated four more years of blissful sinning without responsibility. Not by coincidence, I was converted at the age of twelve.

A similar situation existed in our society twenty-five years ago. Public confidence in our leaders and our institutions permitted them to serve without accounting except in cases of gross malfeasance. All is changed today. Accountability has come of age as public confidence in our leaders and our institutions has turned to doubt and even distrust:

. . . industrialists are called to account for the burning
of high-sulphur coal which causes acid rain,

. . . automakers recall millions of defective new cars,

. . . a leading surgeon is found guilty of negligence in
the death of a patient and required to pay the
family $350,000 in damages,

. . . an accrediting agency issues new standards for
quality which are based upon accountability for
learning outcomes and student achievement.

Thirty-five years ago our president had the full support
of the American people when decisions were made about
our involvement in Korea. Even twenty years ago, we stood
proudly with President Kennedy when he risked war in
setting up the Cuban blockade and still stayed with him
after the Bay of Pigs fiasco. Today, however, the deep
wounds of Vietnam, the revelations of Watergate and the
inability to free the Iranian hostages make us suspicious
of leadership at every level.

Of course, those who must answer are resisting the new
public demand for accountability. One college administrator contends that accountability is a child of the corporate
culture and that we have no business imposing cost-analy-
sis, cost-benefit and cost-effective standards upon the educational enterprise. A corporate executive, in turn, identifies
performance appraisal as a Machiavellian technique con-
cocted by a benevolent autocrat for the purpose of manipu-
lating human behavior.

Accountability has even come of age for clergy. In a recent meeting with a religious book publisher, I asked,
"What is the hot-button in the ministry today?" Without
hesitation, the publisher answered, "Accountability. Ministers are being called to accountability without the standards to judge their effectiveness."

A common reaction against accountability in religious
circles is that measurable standards are easy to develop
and implement when we are dealing with numbers rather

than souls and working toward material rather than spiritual goals. No doubt this is true, and yet it does not mean that we are excused from our responsibility in religion to account for our work to achieve personal growth, religious understanding and spiritual development. Peter Drucker dispels any such notion when he states, *"The purpose of accountability is the development of people."* Within that context, I propose that we advance our understanding and acceptance of accountability from numbers to people, from performance to potential and from material to spiritual outcomes. To rethink our pastoral responsibility for the development of people may well be our growing edge now that accountability has come of age.

ACCOUNTABILITY AS BIBLICAL TRUTH

As a baseline for our discussion, we must recognize that *accountability is a biblical truth,* even though it is a new cause. Human beings have a tendency to advance new causes as if the principle behind the cause had just been discovered. The ebb and flow of "environmentalism" is a case in point. Pollution, waste and the limits of physical resources drove us to the edge of panic in the 1970s. Critics of Christianity blamed the Protestant ethic for creating attitudes that made growth, prosperity and materialism the idols before which our industrial society bowed. Then, Rene Dubos, the father of environmentalism, quieted the critics by writing in his book, *A God Within,* that the stewardship of physical resources is a biblical concept given by God to man in the Garden of Eden.[1] According to Dubos, Christianity has not failed. It is we who have failed to apply the biblical principle of stewardship to our environment.

The sudden interest in accountability has the same flavor. It is advanced as a human concept that has just been discovered. In truth, accountability is nothing more than another turn of the wheel in which the biblical principle of judgment for our ultimate trust and our penultimate task comes front and center once again. Genesis opens with God Himself accounting for the quality of His creative work and pronouncing it "good." Revelation closes with the standard of accounting that no man shall add to or subtract from the Word of God without his name being erased from the Book of Life and he denied entrance into the presence of God. In between Genesis and Revelation is the repeated truth of man's responsibility to God and his brother. Accountability rings from the ethical peak of the Old Testament when Micah speaks: "What does the Lord require of you but to do justly, to love mercy, and walk humbly with your God?" (6:8).

Accountability breathes in every word when Jesus affirms a lawyer's summation of the law and the prophets in a single sentence: "You shall love the Lord your God with all your heart . . . soul . . . mind and your neighbor as yourself'" (Luke 10:27).

If you want to add another dimension to Bible study, take any book of the Scriptures and list the standards of accountability that God reveals to us in it. Of course, add a parallel column for the graces God gives to us to meet His standards. The point is that accountability is biblical truth, not a passing human fancy or a current human discovery.

STANDARDS FOR PASTORAL ACCOUNTABILITY

Jesus Himself gives us a case study of accountability. According to management theorists, a simple cycle of accountability includes goal-setting, feedback and goal-setting once again. Each of these components is present in John 17—Jesus' last recorded prayer before He goes to His passion. Within this lofty prayer are these practical truths about accountability. Jesus accepts responsibility for

> . . . the *goals* He set,
> . . . the *resources* He received,
> . . . the *people* He taught,
> . . . the *attitudes* He communicated,
>   and
> . . . the *example* He left.

These same standards apply to pastors. Through Jesus' final report to His Father, we learn how we are accountable as His disciples for our goals, our resources, our people, our attitudes and our example.

First, we are accountable for the goals we set. Jesus says to His Father, "I have finished the work that You gave Me to do." What an amazing statement! With a ministry so limited in space and so short in time, Jesus must have practiced *one-minute goal-setting* as described in that best-selling, undersized and overpriced book entitled *The One-Minute Manager* by Blanchard and Johnson. You will remember that the idea of *one-minute goal-setting* is to write measurable goals in behavioral terms in less than 250 words on one sheet of paper so that the maximum reading time is 60 seconds. Jesus does better than this. At the beginning of His ministry in Nazareth He outlines His mission, motive, methods, market and mood in just 57 words that take 30 seconds to read.

> The Spirit of the Lord is upon Me,
> Because He has anointed Me to preach the
> gospel to the poor.
> He has sent Me to heal the brokenhearted,
> To preach deliverance to the captives
> And recovery of sight to the blind,
> To set at liberty those who are oppressed,
> To preach the acceptable year of the Lord.

With this public declaration, Jesus dares to set high goals for His ministry and yet they are so specific that He can be held accountable for the results. Our problem is not high goals; they are essential for motivation. The rub comes in our inability to exercise the companion principles of "chunking" and "niching" which are described in another best-selling book, *In Search of Excellence*. [2] "Chunking" is the technique of dividing large tasks into manageable parts. Even though Jesus has the grand purpose of redeeming the world, He "chunks" His ministry by restricting His mission to the poor of the house of Israel, limiting His method to preaching, confining His market to the broken, bruised and bound, and focusing His mood on a note of Jubilee.

"Niching," then, is the responsibility to match His gifts with the goals He has set. In Mark's Gospel, for instance, we see Jesus putting into practice the principle of "niching." In the first half of the Gospel, Jesus is identified as the "Servant of Man" ministering through His preaching, teaching and healing. In the last half of Mark, He gives Himself to His identity as the "Son of Man" who must die to redeem the world. Jesus establishes high and attainable goals for His short-lived ministry. Thus, He can say to the Father, "I have finished the work that You gave Me to do." From His example, we have our standard of accountability as pastors. We are responsible for achieving the goals we set.

Second, we are accountable for the resources we are given. Within the context of John 17 (RSV), Jesus acknowledges the resources that the Father put into His hand to accomplish His work. He is given the Father's "power" (verse 2), the Father's "name" (verse 6) and the Father's "words" (verse 8).

Power is the primary resource for pastoral leadership. Although its definition varies in management literature, power generally refers to the "capacity to influence human behavior in a given direction." Four types of power are identified: *coercive power* is the capacity of the leader to influence the behavior of subordinates by rewards and punishments; *legitimate power* is the authority or the right of the executive to make a request of a subordinate; *expert power* is the superior knowledge of the executive for

problem solving; and *referent power* is the quality of the
character of the executive for influencing behavior. Jesus
has all of these types of power at His disposal. Coercive
power is His because we read that God has given Him
"power over all flesh." Legitimate power is His because
He bears the name of God. Expert power is His because
He knows the Word of God.

Yet, each of these types of power has its drawback. Research shows that coercive power based upon force builds
resistance, legitimate power utilizing names and titles results in temporary compliance and expert power may lead
to commitment only under given circumstances. Notice how
Jesus uses these forms of power. Against demons He does
not hesitate to exercise coercive power. When seeking a
colt upon which to ride into Jerusalem in triumph, He uses
legitimate power in His instruction to His disciples, "Say
that the Son of Man hath need of him." And in verbal
combat with the Pharisees His expert power in knowledge
of the Word of God eventually reduces them to silence.
To fulfill His God-given purpose of bringing eternal life
to men and glorifying His Father (verses 1–4), however,
Jesus relies on referent power or the quality of His character to convince men that His Father is the only true God
and that He is the beloved Son. The result, then, is that
Jesus reports to His Father, "I have glorified Thee on the
earth . . . ," a statement of accountability that tells us
that Jesus is not corrupted by the power He is given. What
a contrast with the statement of Charles Beard, the renowned American historian who, when asked to sum up
his learning of a lifetime in one sentence, answered, "Whom
the gods would destroy, they first make drunk with power."

Human temptation is always to use the power we are
given to glorify ourselves or our systems. Some pastors live
with the temptation to use their power for self-glory; others
are more easily seduced to use their power to glorify the
system. In either case, if an individual or an institution
is glorified, God is not.

I shall never forget the true story about Adolph Hitler. As a puny corporal with a questionable war record, he failed to qualify for a soldier's pension. After his ascent to dictatorial power he ordered the Bureau of Pensions to grant him his monthly allowance. Yet he went to his death in the bunker at Berchtesgaden frustrated by the stonewalling of a bureaucratic process that never responded to his dictatorial demand.

Jesus uses His power to achieve the goals of His ministry but never to glorify Himself or exalt a system. Thus, our second standard of pastoral accountability is that we are responsible to glorify God with the power we are given.

Third, we are accountable for the people with whom we work. In reporting on His finished task Jesus says to the Father, "I have manifested Your name to the men whom You have given Me out of the world" (verse 6). God not only gives Jesus power over all flesh; He also gives Him His Name. By using the power that God gives to Him over all flesh, Jesus finishes the task and demonstrates the value of achievement for His disciples. But achievement is never enough. Studies show that power, even referent power, used only to achieve a given task is usually applied impersonally, impulsively and arbitrarily. Mature leaders, however, have what the theorists call a "socialized power concern," meaning that they identify with people and people identify with them. Those who work with us need a sense of affiliation as well as a sense of achievement.

The name we bear meets our need for affiliation by establishing our identity and defining our commitments. God gives Jesus His Name for this purpose and Jesus in turn reports that He has "kept" His disciples in the Father's Name. They know who they are and He has their commitment.

In the organizational world we are learning the importance of names. Employees who identify with the name of a leader, an organization or a unit of the organization create a more effective work climate in which there is team spirit, a sense of personal responsibility and better group performance.

As corny as it may seem, the Japanese "quality circles" where the employees sing company songs and recite company slogans may have something to teach us. In the best-selling book, *In Search of Excellence,* the authors point out that the best-run companies in America invariably have employees who share the pride of the corporate name.[3] As a person who frequently flies Delta Airlines, I know that Delta has the slogan of a "Family Feeling" among its employees. While our plane was moving away from the terminal in Atlanta, the Delta captain invited us to look out the window to see the new Boeing 767 next to us. With pride he pointed to the name "Delta Spirit" on the airplane and said that it was a thirty-million-dollar gift to the company from the Delta family.

I downplayed his enthusiasm as hype until I returned to the same terminal on a Delta flight at 5 A.M. on Sunday morning. Rumpled and red-eyed, I slouched half-asleep at the terminal with several other noncommunicative passengers waiting for the next flight home. Down the concourse came three pert and pretty Delta stewardesses, obviously the crew for our flight. They turned into a door which I assumed to be a special waiting room, but then, to my surprise, they reappeared holding aloft trays of orange juice and coffee. The whole atmosphere of the terminal was transformed as they demonstrated the Delta "Family Feeling" by passing out refreshments with a smile and a cheery "Good Morning."

Think about the names we bear—the name of our faith, the name of our family, the name of our institution, the name of our job. How do we use the names we bear to develop the people who work with us—affirming their identity, meeting their need for affiliation and engaging their commitment? Jesus said, "I have kept them in Your name . . ." (verse 12)—a standard of accountability for us who are pastors in all our working relationships.

Fourth, we are accountable for the attitudes we communicate. God also gives Jesus the resource of His words to teach the disciples. In His final report, Jesus says, ". . . I have given to them the words which You have given Me" (verse 8). He goes on to say that the disciples received His words, accepted His deity and believed on Him. Through the effective use of the Father's power, Jesus gives the disciples a sense of *achievement.* Through the transfer of the Father's Name, He gives them their sense of *affiliation.* And now through the teaching of the Father's words, He gives them their sense of *autonomy.* The end of effective teaching is always independence for the student to advance and apply human knowledge. In this case, the end of Jesus' teaching is to send the disciples into the world even as the Father has sent Him into the world (verse 18). So, Jesus prays for their freedom by asking that His joy might be fulfilled in them (verse 13). "Joy," in this context, means that the truth of God's Word has been so internalized that the disciples can teach others with inspiration. Like the singer who is set free from the musical score to soar in song, the goal of Jesus' teaching is to see His disciples as independent masters of truth and autonomous artists of communication.

Each of us, then, is a teacher who is accountable for our words and the attitudes we communicate. The key to accountability in teaching is feedback. The advice of *The One-Minute Manager* is sound in advocating one-minute praisings and one-minute reprimands as a teaching-learning process. Once again, research studies show us that there is no greater motivation than high and achievable goals followed by quick, objective and affirmative feedback. Do you remember John Wooden's response to the question, "How do you motivate your basketball players?" Wooden answered, "I catch them doing something right." *The One-Minute Manager* has picked up that principle as the basis for one-minute praisings.[4] Likewise, we need to learn how to lead with one-minute reprimands in which we "eliminate the behavior and keep the person." So the goal of our teaching is to create a climate of "joy" in which our people are free to grow and able to teach others. As pastors we are accountable for the attitudes we communicate.

Fifth, we are accountable for the example we set. After achieving His task and teaching His disciples, Jesus anticipates the magnitude and the risk of their continuing work in the world. Abruptly, He stops praying for them to put Himself back on the line with this commitment, "and for their sakes I sanctify Myself, that they also may be sanctified by the truth" (verse 19). With this final act of dedication, Jesus sets the highest example for the accountable leader.

The book *In Search of Excellence* poses an irony in light of the current loss of public confidence in our leadership. Peters and Waterman, the authors, confess in the preface to the book that they began their research with the assumption that leadership was incidental to the development of corporate excellence. Their assumption proved false immediately. Behind every corporation that met their standard for excellence, they found a legendary leader who personified the ideals of the company, gave priority to people and considered the shaping of values as the primary responsibility of leadership.[5]

Eddie Carlson, Chairman of the Board of United Airlines, is mentioned as one of those legendary leaders in the book. Shortly after he was elected Chairman of United Airlines several years ago, I met him on a flight going from Chicago to Seattle. As usual, I was making my way to a seat in the coach section when I noticed that Eddie was in row 23 seat D just ahead of me. Surprised, I asked, "Eddie, what are you doing back here riding steerage?" He told me that he was spending the first six weeks of his new role traveling around the country to meet personally with the ticket agents, stewardesses, mechanics and baggage handlers of United Airlines. "After all," he said, "if the 'Friendly Skies' is to be more than a slogan, it must begin with me."

On the other side of the ledger is the report that came to us recently from a group of prominent Christian leaders in the nation. In a moment of truth, they confessed that they lacked the depth of spiritual resources needed to respond to the spiritual needs of their people today. Elton Trueblood speaks profound truth when he writes in his book *The New Man for Our Time,* "One cannot give what one does not have."[6]

When all is said and done, our accountability as pastors is personal. If we are to

> . . . finish our task,
> . . . glorify our Father,
> . . . affirm our people,
> . . . teach the Truth
> and
> . . . communicate joy,

we must begin all over again where Jesus started the cycle of accountability. For the sake of those whom we serve and lead, our prayer must be, "I sanctify myself that they also might be sanctified in Truth." For this and for them we are accountable.

XII

Redeeming Our Future

Best-selling books signal the thoughts and feelings, values and attitudes, hopes and fears of our people. In the 1980s, John Naisbitt's book *Megatrends* has set the pace. Not only is *Megatrends* the best seller of the decade, but it is on the shelves of more libraries in the nation than any other single volume, including the Kings James Version of the Bible! People talk about it over coffee, read it on airplanes, organize discussion groups around it and relate its observations to business, education and government.

Naisbitt subtitles his book, "Ten New Directions Transforming Our Lives." Simply put, we are moving:

> . . . from an Industrial Society to an Information Society,
> . . . from forced technology industries to Hi-Tech, Hi-Touch human needs,
> . . . from a national economy to a world economy,
> . . . from short-term to long-term planning,

   . . . from centralized to decentralized authority,
   . . . from institutional to self-help programs,
   . . . from representative to participatory democracy,
   . . . from hierarchies to networking,
   . . . from North to South
       and
   . . . from either/or to multiple options.[1]

Behind these megatrends is Naisbitt's foundational thesis. We are in a "time of parenthesis" between the dying Industrial Society and the dawning Informational Society. Energy, wealth and power are being redefined. The physical resources of coal, oil and uranium that fueled the Industrial Society are giving way to the intellectual resources of facts, ideas and values which will fuel the Information Society. Even now, we feel the trauma of transition in the decline of heavy industry, the inadequacy of our school systems, the proliferation of media options and the startling fact that a majority of our gross national product is being spent in the hi-tech industries of information and communication. Rippling through our society, then, are ten trends that are literally transforming the direction of our lives.

What has this to do with ministry? In one way or another, each of the megatrends leading to an Information Society has implications for the current preparation and long-term development of the pastor. The church is always tested in a time of transition and the role of the pastor is usually at the point of test. To retreat into the secure patterns of the past, according to Naisbitt, is like dinosaurs mating. Or, to ignore the megatrends is like a dodo bird waiting for the weather to change. Our only option is to ask, "How do these megatrends affect our ministry?" and "How do we minister in a time of transition?" Ten capsule comments will lead us into our future.

FROM AN INDUSTRIAL TO AN INFORMATIONAL SOCIETY

Information is the basis for reformations and revolutions. A weak comparison can be drawn between the invention of the printing press in the sixteenth century and the invention of the computer in the twentieth century. Out of what Marshall McLuhan called the "Gutenberg Galaxy," the Bible was put in the hands of common people. The Reformation resulted. Now, in the "Electronic Galaxy" of the twentieth century, the amount and speed of information available to the general populace are being multiplied millions of times. Another revolution is in the making. Although the full impact of an Information Society is yet ahead of us, we are already victims of "information overload"—bombarded by more facts, ideas and opinions than we can process. We are also victims of "information mush." At the center of a crossfire from many different information sources, we find it difficult to sort out right from wrong and truth from error.

In response to the "overload" and "mush" of the coming Information Society, we need an *authoritative ministry*. Naisbitt says that in a time of transition between eras of human civilization, people need structure—something to hang on to. An authoritative ministry is literate, articulate and biblical. Or as E. Stanley Jones said, "We must prepare to preach with one eye on the Bible and the other on the newspaper." When Jesus preached in the synagogue, the people exclaimed, "He speaks with authority." Rather than droning on with a complicated, opinionated and irrelevant recitation of the Law as the Pharisees did, Jesus preached the Word of God with clarity of thought and relevance to the people.

Computers and television sets may be our mechanical Pharisees—overloading us with information and mushing on the truth. If so, the essence of an *authoritative ministry* is biblical preaching that helps us sort out relevant information and leads us through the mush to the Truth.

FROM HI-TECH TO HI-TOUCH

Technology glorifies the machine and invades the functions of the human mind. As each new generation of computers raises the level of sophistication in processing information, people are not only displaced from their jobs but feel as if they have been dehumanized by a machine. Thus, Naisbitt refutes the vision of an "electronic cottage" in which people will stay home and do their work by computer. Early evidence shows that people will forsake the efficiency of the machine to be in touch with other people. Projecting this evidence into the future, Naisbitt sees the need for "Hi-Touch" human relationships rising with each new level of "Hi-Tech" sophistication.

Evangelical Christianity is already on the front-edge of "Hi-Touch" needs. Relational theology leads the laity, relational books are best sellers, relational preachers are most popular and relational churches are the growing churches. The dangers of these "Hi-Touch" ministries overriding the need for "Hi-Truth" preaching are well-known. Michael Novak has put it succinctly in his warning that evangelical Christianity may be weakened by "bad faith, cheap grace and shallow piety." Even greater is the danger of personality cults and ecstatic religious experiences as radical responses to "Hi-Touch" needs. Yet if the church is to be responsive to the groping for human contact among people who feel displaced and dehumanized by high technology, *the ministry must be relational* —a balance of Hi-Truth with Hi-Touch.

From a National Economy to a World Economy

Narrow nationalism depends upon limited information in the hands of a few people. As more information becomes more available to the masses, a world perspective develops. Even now, the protectionist walls of the old nationalistic economy are breaking down. Bumper stickers reading "Made in the U.S.A." are fast disappearing. Very few automobiles are exclusively "foreign" or "domestic." According to Naisbitt, the more accurate bumper sticker would read, "Global Car," representing the new interdependence of a world economy. Information is tying the world together, not just in the making of cars and the economics of multinational corporations, but in social expectations, diplomatic realities and spiritual hunger.

One of the undying strengths of the church is its world vision and world witness. Yet, there is always the danger of holding on to an antiquated view of the world and an obsolete strategy for witness. A "global" view of our changing world will quickly bring us up to date and project us into the future. We will know that we are fellow travelers on a speeding, shrinking, interlocking and explosive planet called Earth. We will know that our concept of world mission cannot be limited to the foreign field at the expense of domestic need. We will know that our world strategy cannot be selected just for those who are most receptive to the gospel. We will know that our world witness cannot be decided by moral issues that are of our own choosing. We will know that our world task includes the cause of justice in social structures as well as mercy in human relief. Isolation from these realities behind the protection of a narrow religious nationalism is not our privilege. If we are to be "Global Christians" we need the perspective of a *global* ministry, beginning in the local church.

FROM SHORT- TO LONG-TERM PLANNING

Limited information necessitates short-term, frequent planning. Now, however, as we are gaining instant, worldwide communication and developing the tools for predicting future trends, long-term planning becomes an obligation, not a luxury. In personal terms, the most immediate impact of long-term planning is the new requirement for lifelong learning. Educators, however, are still talking about "terminal degrees" that prepare a student for a lifetime career. The Information Society renders this viewpoint obsolete and dangerous. New knowledge in all fields of study make lifelong learning inevitable. In fact, three or four intensive periods of educational updating, and sometimes retraining, will be required of professionals in the lifetime of their careers.

Ministers in the Age of Information must be lifelong learners. Our vision for ministry must include continuing education throughout a lifetime and periods of intensive study for rethinking and reworking our professional role. Paralleling this new perception of ministry must be curricular reform in Christian colleges and seminaries. Terminal degrees must give way to lifelong professional development, of which degrees are a part. Curriculum must shift from a static and segmented classical learning to a dynamic and integrated world view. Teaching-learning, then, will aim toward effective ministerial outcomes in the contemporary world rather than traditional answers for the academic world. There is no option. Megatrends bring together *lifelong learning* with the lifetime ministry.

FROM CENTRALIZATION TO DECENTRALIZATION

Centralized authority depends upon privileged information accumulated in the hands of a limited number of people. In the forthcoming Information Society, however, the direction of communication will be reversed. Information will be distributed outwardly toward the masses rather than inwardly toward the few. Authority will move with the information. Old centers of power will be threatened by smaller, local and decentralized units of power created by people with shared information. Anticipating this change, the authors of the book *Corporate Cultures* predict that the organization of the future will be modeled after McDonald's restaurants.[2] At the center of the organization is a leadership that functions as a resource for shared values, education and quality control. All other aspects of organizational authority are distributed to individual franchises across the world. Yet wherever the sign of the Golden Arches is seen, the consumer is assured of Quality, Value, Service and Cleanliness.

The authority for ministry has also depended upon privileged information accumulated at a center of power. Denominational headquarters and ecclesiastical officers have been the point of control. Now they are being challenged by the redistribution of information to local churches where effective ministry requires adequate authority. Thus, McDonald's may be the model for the church of the future. Rather than continuing to accumulate power at the center of the organization, the heads and headquarters of the church should become resource units for shared values, educational services and quality control in local churches. The Age of Information requires a *decentralized* ministry with authority at the point of function.

FROM INSTITUTIONAL TO SELF-HELP PROGRAMS

Closely aligned with the forces of decentralization is the megatrend moving from institutional help to self-help programs. In the past, we have come to depend upon help from public and private institutions for needs ranging from health and safety to education and religion. Not unlike the Romans who were kept subservient by "bread and circuses," our strength of character has been weakened by the expectation that we are "entitled" to both protection and privilege from our institutions. Cutbacks in federal funding have been a mixed blessing. While neglecting some of the poor, hungry and sick who have fallen through the "safety net," the cutbacks have challenged citizens to create self-help programs for the needy. Whether food banks, health centers, counseling agencies or street shelters, there is evidence that self-help is on the rise. More than that, followup studies of institutional help for human service needs are showing that professional intervention may hurt more than it heals. Consequently, we are learning that self-help may be the best path to self-healing for problems of health, education and welfare.

Spiritual self-help is not a contradiction in terms. In the Reformation, we moved away from the position that only the priests could pronounce absolution for sin to the self-help cry of the sinner appealing directly to God. Now, in the emerging Age of Information, we do not rely exclusively upon the preacher to give us the Word of God. Hundreds of self-help resources for the study and understanding of the Word are available through books, manuals, cassettes and other media. Ministers cannot resist these trends. An effective ministry in the Information Society requires an unusual sensitivity to the needs of people and a pastoral response that will help them help themselves. A *self-help* ministry is the wave of the future.

FROM REPRESENTATIVE TO PARTICIPATORY DEMOCRACY

Instant communication and comprehensive information change the very nature of the governing process. When information is slow, selective and limited, the populace has to depend upon political parties and elected representatives to carry their cause. But when information is instant, open and unlimited, everyone has an opinion to voice and a vote to cast. No longer are people willing to let others make decisions for them. Especially in matters where their welfare is directly concerned, they demand participation in the decision-making process. In the political realm, for instance, citizens have risen to power through initiatives and referenda that have limited or permitted taxation, nuclear plants, gambling and gay rights. In the economic realm, informed buyers have created a "new consumerism" that demands quality and service in commercial products. Instant and unlimited information is the power base from which these citizens' groups operate. Representative democracy is still alive, but even our elected officials are being called into new accountability by informed and concerned constituencies.

Because the church is a body of volunteer members that emphasizes preaching and teaching, we might expect it to be a model of participatory democracy. History tells us otherwise. Even though the Reformation broke down the wall

of separation between sacred and secular worlds, a line
of demarcation still divides clergy and laity. Many of the
most successful churches are built around charismatic and
authoritarian personalities; many other churches involve
their members in administrative decisions, but not in matters of doctrine and discipline; and many more churches
only selectively engage the gifts of laity in the ministry
of the church.

The word is out. Participatory democracy will spill over
from the culture to the church. Parishioners will expect
to be involved in the decisions that represent their personal,
social and spiritual welfare. They will not buy a preacher's
mandate on how to vote, spend money and raise a family
without a voice in the discussion. "Thus saith the Lord"
will still be the message they expect to hear but not without
critical testing to determine whether the authority comes
from God or man. The megatrend toward participatory democracy tells us that the pastoral leader of the future will
develop a *participatory* ministry, involving the laity in
church policy, in hearing them out in matters of doctrine
and discipline—and utilizing their potential for the work
and witness of the church.

FROM HIERARCHIES TO NETWORKING

Instant, open and unlimited information not only decen-
tralizes authority, fosters self-help and encourages participation in decision-making, it also breaks down hierarchical
control. Hierarchies are characterized by power rising to
a focus at the top of the organization and exercising control
over all facets of life. Once again, such power and control
depends upon privileged information and selective communication to the people at the "grass roots." Hierarchies,
then, lose power and control when people have access to
instant, open and unlimited information. In their place,
networks of special interest spring up to challenge the hierarchy. The Moral Majority, for instance, is a network of

special interests whose leader, a fundamentalist preacher, is quick to point out that the membership crosses over religious, regional, economic and ethnic lines and comes together under the common cause of traditional, conservative values. Other groups of special interest are discovering the power of networking. Not insignificantly, politicians in large cities go out of their way to win the vote of networks that range all the way from senior citizens to gay rights advocates.

Ministers still tend to think of the church in hierarchical terms. Examples are competition with parachurch ministries, opposition to special interest groups not under the aegis of the church and duplication of ministries in local church empires. In each case, the issue comes down to personal egos, limited dollars and hierarchical protection. Reality tells us that networks of special ministries and religious causes outside of the institutional church are here to stay. Rather than contesting, opposing or duplicating these networks, ministers must learn to work with them. How, for instance, can the local church serve the converts of parachurch ministries, utilize the resources of specialized ministries and cooperate with other churches in meeting human service needs? Evangelical Christians are notorious for their failure to work together because of a hierarchical mindset that is falsely justified by theological distinctions. In the Information Society, networks will replace empires and the biblical principle of stewardship will require ministers to develop *cooperative* rather than competitive ministries.

FROM NORTH TO SOUTH

Heavy industry depends upon proximity to physical resources and transportation centers to be economical and successful. The Information Industry is just the opposite— it is light, mobile and nonpolluting. Therefore, while heavy industry has been destined to develop in the North and

Northeast, high technology has grown up in the more favorable climates of the South, Southwest and West. Like tipping the table of the nation, people are moving from North to South and taking with them the centers of economic and political power. According to Naisbitt, California, Texas and Florida are now the megastates of the future.

More than economics is involved in the North-South migration. Regional differences in the demographics of age, race and ethnic origin as well as differences in personal, social and spiritual values mean that people who move from North to South literally change worlds. Notably, the megastates of California, Texas and Florida are leaders in the split-culture between young and old, migrant and native, rich and poor, educated and noneducated, English and non-English-speaking people. One might add that these states also represent great divergence between spiritual and secular values.

For the church that is left behind in the North or the church that is moving to the South, the challenge is to minister in the demographic diversity and value contradictions of a fast-moving, fun-loving, materialistic and affluent culture. Much has been said and written about cross-cultural communication for the church in foreign missions. The same principles will have to be applied to the ministry of the church in a Hi-Tech world. How do we communicate across the generational lines of young and old, the educational lines of schooled and unschooled, the economic lines of rich and poor, the linguistic lines of English and non-English-speaking people, the racial lines of colored and white and the value lines of spiritual and secular? In response to the megatrend of migration from North to South, our ministry must be *cross-cultural.*

FROM EITHER/OR TO MULTIPLE OPTIONS

Limited information forces our choices into either/or categories. Naisbitt reminds us of the simple world in which we chose to marry or not marry, work or not work, vote

or not vote, go to college or not go to college, attend church
or not attend church, buy a Ford or a Chevy and choose
chocolate or vanilla ice cream cones. All of this has changed.
We now have multiple options in marriage, family, employment, education, religion, automobiles, entertainment and
even ice cream. A Russian exile who spent years trying
to get out of the USSR confessed that he preferred his home-
land because he was frustrated by the freedom of too many
options in America. Perhaps he is a prophet. Just around
the corner in the Information Age, we will have ninety-
eight cable television channels from which to choose.
The options will range from X-rated movies to computer
shopping.

Ministers are conditioned to either/or preaching and
teaching. The nature of the gospel itself is stated in either/
or terms—sheep or goats, lost or found, life or death, God
or Satan, heaven or hell. These eternal choices will not
change. The problem, however, is the tendency to carry
over an either/or mindset into more temporal decisions
for which there are multiple options. If we try to force
an either/or choice upon personal decisions about marriage,
family, employment, education, entertainment, politics and
social issues, we confuse our responsibility for preaching
and teaching. "Thus saith the Lord" is still the keynote
for preaching in an Information Society, but "Come let
us reason together" is the call for biblical teaching in an
age of multiple options. Ministers who have either/or answers for every multiple option shortchange their parishioners. When the next option comes around, the people
lack the ethical tools to work through their own moral
choices. Therefore, in an Information Age, we need a *teaching* ministry that equips Christians for ethical, biblical
decision-making.

TRUTH IN MINISTRY

A realistic job preview for the minister in the Informational Age has been written. It is not just formid-

able, it is well-nigh impossible. Imagine the following ad:

WANTED
Ministers for the Information Society

Applicant must . . .
          . . . preach with authority,
          . . . relate to human need,
          . . . see global concerns,
          . . . plan lifelong learning,
          . . . foster self-help programs,
          . . . cooperate with network ministries,
          . . . facilitate lay participation,
          . . . teach for ethical decisions.

The missing dimension is the requirement for a *Spirit-
filled* ministry. Emphasis upon the work of the Holy Spirit
in the life of the minister has been upon cleansing, comfort-
ing, nurturing, leading and empowering. Without losing
these distinctive works of the Spirit, we cannot neglect His
role in helping us discern the truth, which is our primary
need as we enter into the issues of the Information Age.

Jesus promises, "When He, the Spirit of Truth, has come,
He will guide you into all truth" (John 16:13). Is this not
the discerning Spirit that we need when bombarded by
bits and pieces of truth from every direction and weighted
down by information overload?

Jesus also promises that He, the Spirit of Truth, will
convince the world of sin, righteousness and judgment. Is
not this the conviction that we need to make spiritual
choices out of moral mush? Convinced of the reality of sin,
we will not fall easy prey to the false optimism that man
is good or redemption is easy. Convinced of the reality of
righteousness, we will not give up on the world or succumb
to the despair that fails to see the potential of redeemed
humanity. Convinced of the reality of judgment, we will
never let arrogance rule our human efforts or lose the sense
of humor that keeps us from taking ourselves too seriously.

Perhaps this is why Jesus promises that the Spirit of Truth will "show us things to come." Spirit-filled ministers are natural futurists. Is this not our need as we are in a time of transition? We need to see the future, guard against its dangers and see hope in its arrival. Spirit-filled ministers are not only human realists and natural futurists, but spiritual optimists.

Naisbitt's final sentence in *Megatrends* is the exuberant exclamation, "My God, what a fantastic time to be alive!"[3] If a secular prophet can voice this hope, how much more should we, ministers of the Good News, greet the dawning of the Information Society with the jubilant shout, "Thank God, what a time to be a pastor!"

Endnotes

Chapter II

1. Keith Miller, *The Becomers* (Waco, Texas: Word Books, 1973) 162.
2. Elizabeth O'Connor, *The Eighth Day of Creation* (Waco, Texas: Word Books, 1972) 48.
3. Peter Drucker, *The Effective Executive* (New York: Harper & Row, 1967) 1–2.

Chapter III

1. Fred Smith, *You and Your Network* (Waco, Texas: Word Books, 1984) 80.
2. Parker Palmer, *To Know As We Are Known/A Spirituality of Education* (San Francisco: Harper & Row, 1983) 48.
3. *Ibid.,* 35.
4. *Ibid.*
5. *Ibid.,* 31.
6. Gary A. Yukl, *Leadership in Organizations* (Englewood Cliffs, New Jersey: Prentice Hall, Inc., 1981) 29.

Chapter IV

1. Howard A. Snyder, *The Community of the King* (Downers Grove, Illinois: Inter-Varsity Press, 1977) 61.
2. James David Barbour, *The Presidential Character* (Englewood Cliffs, New Jersey: Prentice-Hall, 1972).
3. Warren Bennis and Burton Nanus, *Leaders* (New York: Harper & Row, 1985) 55–62.

Chapter V

1. Meyer Friedman and Ray H. Rosenman, *Type A Behavior and Your Heart* (New York: Fawcett Crest Books, 1974).
2. Herbert J. Freudenberger, *Burnout: The High Cost of High Achievement* (Garden City, New York: Doubleday, 1981).
3. G. Lloyd Rediger, *Coping with Clergy Burnout* (Valley Forge: Judson Press, 1982).
4. Donald Demaray, *Watch Out for Burnout* (Grand Rapids: Baker Book House, 1983).
5. Bruce Larson, *There's a Lot More to Health Than Not Being Sick* (Waco, Texas: Word Books, 1981).
6. Jerry Edelwich, *Burn-out: Stages of Disillusionment in the Helping Professions* (New York: Human Sciences Press, 1980) 15.
7. Freudenberger, *Burnout: High Cost*, 110.
8. *Ibid.*
9. Georgia Harkness, *The Dark Night of the Soul* (New York: Abingdon-Cokesbury Press, 1945).
10. D. G. Kehl, "Burnout: The Risk of Reaching Too High," *Christianity Today* (November 20, 1981) 27.
11. Erma Bombeck, *Aunt Erma's Cope Book* (New York: Fawcett, 1981) 180.
12. Wayne Oates, *Workaholics, Make Laziness Work for You* (Garden City, New York: Doubleday & Company, Inc., 1979) 115–125.
13. Ayala M. Pines and Elliott Aronson, *Burnout: From Tedium to Personal Growth* (New York: The Free Press, 1981) 45–61.

Chapter VII

1. E. F. Shumacher, *Good Work* (New York: Harper Colophon Books, 1979) 69–70.
2. John W. Gardner, *No Easy Victories* (New York: Harper & Row, 1968) 46.
3. Thomas J. Peters and Robert H. Waterman, *In Search of Excellence* (New York: Warner Books, 1982) 66–67.
4. E. Stanley Jones, *The Divine Yes* (Nashville: Abingdon Press, 1975) 34.

5. F. F. Bruce, *The New International Commentary on the New Testament: Acts* (Grand Rapids: Wm. B. Eerdmans Publishing Co., 1979) 130.
6. Jones, *Divine Yes*, 148.

Chapter VIII

1. James MacGregor Burns, *Leadership* (New York: Harper & Row, 1979).
2. David Reisman, *The Lonely Crowd* (New York: Yale University Press, 1950).
3. Drucker, *Effective Executive*, 15–16.

Chapter IX

1. Norman Cousins, *Human Options* (New York: W. W. Norton & Company, 1981) 23.

Chapter X

1. Kenneth Blanchard and Spencer Johnson, *The One-Minute Manager* (New York: William Morrow and Company, Inc., 1982) 28.
2. John Naisbitt, *Megatrends* (New York: Warner Books, 1982) 85.
3. Michael Maccoby, *The Gamesman* (New York: Simon and Schuster, 1976).

Chapter XI

1. Rene Dubos, *A God Within* (New York: Charles Scribner's Sons, 1972) 45.
2. Peters and Waterman, *In Search of Excellence*, 126–134, 182–186.
3. *Ibid.*, 101–103.
4. Blanchard and Johnson, *The One-Minute Manager*, 76–96.
5. Peters and Waterman, *In Search of Excellence*, 26.
6. Elton Trueblood, *The New Man for Our Time* (New York: Harper & Row, 1970) 79.

Chapter XII

1. Naisbitt, *Megatrends*, 1–2.
2. Terence A. Deal and Allan A. Kennedy, *Corporate Cultures* (Reading, Massachusetts: Addison-Wesley Publishing Company, 1982) 193–194.
3. Naisbitt, *Megatrends*, 252.

Bibliography

Anderson, James D. *The Management of Ministry.* San Francisco: Harper & Row, 1978.

Barbour, James David. *The Presidential Character.* Englewood Cliffs, New Jersey: Prentice-Hall, 1972.

Bennis, Warren and Burton Nanus. *Leaders.* New York: Harper & Row, 1985.

Blanchard, Kenneth and Spencer Johnson. *The One-Minute Manager.* New York: William Morrow and Company, Inc., 1982.

Bombeck, Erma. *Aunt Erma's Cope Book.* New York: Fawcett, 1981.

Bromley, Geoffrey William. *Christian Ministry.* Grand Rapids: Wm. B. Eerdmans Publishing Co., 1960.

Brown, Stephen W. *Where the Action Is.* Old Tappan, New Jersey: Fleming H. Revell Co., 1971.

Bruce, F. F. *The New International Commentary on the New Testament: Acts.* Grand Rapids: Wm. B. Eerdmans Publishing Co., 1979.

Burns, James MacGregor. *Leadership.* New York: Harper & Row, 1979.

Caemmerer, Richard R. *Feeding and Leading.* St. Louis: Concordia Publishing House, 1962.

Calkins, Raymond. *Romance of the Ministry.* Boston: The Pilgrim Press, 1944.

Coburn, John B. *Minister: Man in the Middle.* New York: Macmillan, 1963.

Colson, Charles. *Loving God.* Grand Rapids: Zondervan, 1983.

Conference on Motivation for the Ministry. Louisville: Southern Baptist Theological Seminary, 1959.

Cousins, Norman. *Human Options.* New York: W. W. Norton & Company, 1981.

Deal, Terence A. and Allan A. Kennedy. *Corporate Cultures.* Reading, Massachusetts: Addison-Wesley Publishing Company, 1982.

Demaray, Donald. *Watch Out for Burnout.* Grand Rapids: Baker Book House, 1983.

Dittes, James E. *Minister on the Spot.* Philadelphia: Pilgrim Press, 1970.

Dubos, Rene. *A God Within.* New York: Charles Scribner's Sons, 1972.

Drucker, Peter. *The Effective Executive.* New York: Harper & Row, 1967.

Edelwich, Jerry. *Burn-out: Stages of Disillusionment in the Helping Professions.* New York: Human Sciences Press, 1980.

Floyd, William A. *Your Future As a Minister.* New York: R. Rosen Press, 1969.

Freudenberger, Herbert J. and Geraldine Richelson. *Burnout: The Hight Cost of High Achievement.* Garden City, New York: Doubleday, 1981.

Friedman, Meyer and Ray H. Rosenman. *Type A Behavior and Your Heart.* New York: Fawcett Crest Books, 1974.

Gardner, John W. *No Easy Victories.* New York: Harper & Row, 1968.

Gibson, Charles A. *First Things in the Ministry.* Berne, Indiana: Economy Printing Concern, Inc., 1966.

Harbaugh, Gary L. *The Pastor As Person.* Minneapolis: Augsburg Publishing House, 1984.

Harkness, Georgia. *The Dark Night of the Soul.* New York: Abingdon-Cokesbury Press, 1945.

Harris, Gordon E. *Ministry Renewed.* London: S.C.M. Press, 1968.

Hunt, Richard A. *The Christian As Minister.* Nashville: United Methodist Church, 1977.

James, Eric. *Odd Man Out: The Shape of the Ministry Today.* London: Hodder and Stoughton, 1962.

Jenkins, Daniel Thomas. *The Gift of Ministry.* London: Faber and Faber, 1947.

Johnson, Daniel L. *Starting Right, Staying Strong: A Guide to Effective Ministry.* New York: Pilgrim Press, 1983.

Johnson, Merle Allison. *How to Be Happy in the Non-Electric Church.* Nashville: Abingdon Press, 1979.

Jones, E. Stanley. *The Divine Yes.* Nashville: Abingdon Press, 1975.

Jones, Ilion T. *Pastor: The Man and His Ministry.* Philadelphia: Westminster Press, 1961.

Jones, Lloyd and David Martyn. *Preaching and Preachers.* London: Hodder and Stoughton, 1971.

Kehl, D. G. "Burnout: The Risk of Reaching Too High," *Christianity Today,* November 20, 1981, 26–28.

Kemper, Robert G. *The New Shape of Ministry: Taking Accountability Seriously.* Nashville: Abingdon, 1979.

Lawson, A. B. *John Wesley and the Christian Ministry: The Sources and Development of His Opinions and Practice.* London: S.P.C.K., 1963.

Maccoby, Michael. *The Gamesman.* New York: Simon and Schuster, 1976.

McCutcheon, James N. *Pastoral Ministry.* Nashville: Abingdon, 1979.

MacDonald, Murdo Ewen. *Call to Communicate.* Edinburgh: Saint Andrew Press, 1975.

Miller, Keith. *The Becomers.* Waco, Texas: Word Books, 1973.

Mills, Edgar Wendell and John P. Koval. *Stress in the Ministry.* Washington, D.C.: Ministries Studies Board, 1971.

Naisbitt, John. *Megatrends.* New York: Warner Books: 1982.

Niles, D. T. *The Preacher's Calling to Be Servant.* New York: Harper, 1959.

Oates, Wayne. *Workaholics, Make Laziness Work for You.* Garden City, New York: Doubleday & Company, Inc., 1979.

O'Connor, Elizabeth. *The Eighth Day of Creation.* Waco, Texas: Word Books, 1972.

Palmer, Parker. *To Know As We Are Known/A Spirituality of Education.* San Francisco: Harper & Row, 1983.

Pastor X. *How to Murder a Minister.* Old Tappan, New Jersey: Fleming H. Revell, 1970.

Paul, Robert S. *Ministry.* Grand Rapids: Wm. B. Eerdmans Publishing Co., 1965.

Peters, Thomas J. and Robert H. Waterman. *In Search of Excellence.* New York: Warner Books, 1982.

Pines, Ayala M. and Elliott Aronson. *Burnout: From Tedium to Personal Growth.* New York: The Free Press, 1981.

Pym, Thomas Wentworth. *Parson's Dilemmas.* Milwaukee, Wisconsin: Morehouse, 1930.

Ramsey, Arthur Michael. *The Christian Priest Today.* New York: Morehouse Barlow, 1972.

Rediger, G. Lloyd. *Coping with Clergy Burnout.* Valley Forge: Judson Press, 1982.

Reisman, David. *The Lonely Crowd.* New York: Yale University Press, 1950.

Schuette, Walter E. *The Minister's Personal Guide.* New York: Harper Brothers, 1953.

Schumacher, E. F. *Good Work.* New York: Harper Colophon Books, 1979.

Shoemaker, Samuel M. *Beginning Your Ministry.* New York: Harper & Row, 1963.

Smith, Donald P. *Clergy in the Cross Fire: Coping with Role Conflicts in the Ministry.* Philadelphia: Westminster Press, 1973.

Smith, Fred. *You and Your Network.* Waco, Texas: Word Books, 1984.

Snyder, Howard A. *The Community of the King.* Downers Grove, Illinois: Inter-Varsity Press, 1977.

Southard, Samuel. *Pastoral Authority in Personal Relationships.* Nashville: Abingdon Press, 1969.

Stacey, John. *About the Ministry.* London: Epworth Press, 1967.

Stewart, Charles William. *Person and Profession: Career Development in the Ministry.* Nashville: Abingdon Press, 1974.

Strain, Dudley. *The Measure of a Minister.* St. Louis: Bethany Press, 1964.

Switzer, David K. *Pastor, Preacher, Person: Developing a Pastoral Ministry in Depth.* Nashville: Abingdon Press, 1979.

Trueblood, Elton. *The New Man for Our Time.* New York: Harper & Row, 1970.

Walker, W. R. *Ministering Ministry.* Cincinnati: The Standard Publishing Company, 1938.

Wedel, Theodore O. *Ministers of Christ.* New York: Seabury Press, 1964.

Weed, Michael R. *The Minister and His Work.* Austin, Texas: Sweet Publishing Company, 1970.

Wright, Frank. *The Pastoral Nature of the Ministry.* London: S.C.M. Press, 1980.

Yohn, David Waite. *The Contemporary Preacher and His Task.* Grand Rapids: Wm. B. Eerdmans Publishing Co., 1969.

Yukl, Gary A. *Leadership in Organizations.* Englewood Cliffs, New Jersey: Prentice Hall, Inc., 1981.